AMERICAN
Cattle Trails
East & West

Books for young people by Marian T. Place

AMERICAN CATTLE TRAILS
EAST & WEST

•

BUCKSKINS AND BUFFALO
The Story of the Yellowstone River

AMERICAN
Cattle Trails
East & West

BY MARIAN T. PLACE

ILLUSTRATED BY GIL WALKER

HOLT, RINEHART AND WINSTON

NEW YORK   CHICAGO   SAN FRANCISCO

To
Marjorie Moores

Contents

Vancouver

WASH.

MONTANA

Astoria

Columbia R.

Snake R.

OREGON

Walla Walla

Baker City

Boise

IDAHO

Helena

MONIDA PASS

Virginia City

11

Missouri

Yellowstone R.

NORTH DAKOTA

MINNESOTA

MIC

WISCONSIN

CALIFORNIA

NEVADA

Fort Hall

10

WYOMING

SOUTH DAKOTA

IOWA

Milwau

Salt Lake City

UTAH

Cheyenne

COLORADO

Fort Laramie

Ogalalla

NEBRASKA

Platte R.

Omaha

ILLIN

Sacramento

San Francisco

Monterey

Colorado R.

Denver

7

KANSAS

Arkansas R.

Dodge City

8

MISSOURI

Kansas City

Abilene

Newton

Wichita

Grand R.

Sedalia

Fort Scott

Baxter Springs

4

San Diego

9

ARIZONA

NEW MEXICO

Santa Fe

TEXAS

OKLAHOMA

Canadian R.

N. Canadian R.

Cimarron R.

Fort Gibson

Fort Smith

Little Rock

Fort Sumner

Fort Griffin

DOAN'S CROSSING

Fort Worth

RED RIVER STATION

ARKANSAS

LOUISIANA

MEXICO

Pecos R.

Rio Grande

6

Belton

Colorado R.

Brazos R.

Trinity R.

Sabine R.

Red R.

New Orl

Mississippi

San Antonio

5

MATAGORDA ISLAND

CANADA

MAINE

VT.

N.H.

KITTATINNY MT.

1

Boston

MASS.

CONN.

R.I.

N.Y.

Susquehanna R.

PA.

N.J.

MICHIGAN

TUSCARORA MT.

BLUE MT.

Harrisburg

OHIO

Pittsburgh

2

MD.

DELAWARE BAY

ANA

DEL.

W. VA.

VA.

Ohio R.

Richmond

KENTUCKY

3

BERLAND GAP

NORTH CAROLINA

N.

S. CAROLINA

GEORGIA

ALABAMA

le

Tallahassee

St. Augustine

FLORIDA

KEY

1   Bay State Cow Path

2   Three Mountain Trail

3   Daniel Boone's Wilderness Road

4   Texas Road or Osage Trace

5   Chisholm Trail

6   Western Trail

7   Texas Trail

8   Goodnight-Loving Trail

9   California Trail

10   Oregon Trail

11   Northern Trail

1

First Cattle in the New World

Texas, New Mexico, Arizona and Florida

The cattle moved slowly across the sun-drenched land, grazing on the brittle grass. They stirred a column of dust with their cloven hoofs as they pulled farther and farther north, away from their home ground deep in central Mexico. The fiercely-proud Francisco Vásquez de Coronado rode ahead of them, resplendent but sweltering in gold and silver-plated armor and plumed helmet. The Spanish grandee was avid for gold and glory, and determined to find both on this exploration into the New World. Accompanying him was a bold party of mounted adventurers. The soldiers trudged along on foot, armed with arquebuses and lances. They sweated profusely under their breast plates, coats of mail or heavy leather jackets. There were also a few priests, and captive Indian and Mexican laborers to tend to the camp chores, and the band of sheep and the five hundred head of beef cattle.

The leader of Coronado's herd could not be hurried. He was a fine steer—big, black, strong, intelligent, with polished horns set forward to kill, above a long head and a narrow sullen face. The *vaqueros,* or Mexican riders, did not shout at him as they rode effortlessly alongside the cattle. They knew well his long trim legs could outrun their horses. Nor did they prod him, knowing the injury and death his horns could wreak.

His forebears, bulls and cows cut out from a royal Spanish herd, had been brought to Santo Domingo in the West Indies by Columbus on his second voyage to the New World, in 1493. After these cattle had multiplied on the lush vegetation, some had been transported to Cuba. In 1521 Gregorio de Villa-Lobos brought several to Mexico, then called New Spain. Later, while pushing his conquest of Mexico, Hernando Cortés established a hacienda there, and called it Cuernavaca (horn of a cow). He stocked it with Spanish

cattle. This herd also increased. Then more cattle were brought over by other Spanish settlers.

Thus by 1540 when Coronado set out on his unlucky search for fabled cities of gold, he had no difficulty in obtaining five hundred head to provide fresh meat and hides for his expedition. He had plenty of horses too because the Spaniards, having learned ages before to use horses in tending cattle, had brought many to Mexico. After many months on the march, Coronado led his followers up through present-day New Mexico and Arizona, and finally into a region later known as Texas. These were the first cattle to set foot on the future United States.

Coronado never found the golden cities he sought. He and his ever-dwindling company plodded wearily as far west as the Grand Canyon of the Colorado River and as far east as Kansas, before a small band of ragged, emaciated survivors returned empty-handed to Mexico. Coronado would gain everlasting fame for this dogged

exploration. Ironically, although he found no treasure, he left us one. Those first beeves he introduced to America were the source of a golden legacy. It would swell to gigantic proportions and weave one of the most exciting, complex stories of American pioneering and enterprise, that of the movement of millions of cattle over trails that eventually criss-crossed the entire United States.

The fate of the cattle that strayed from Coronado's herd while trailing through present-day New Mexico, Arizona, and Texas can never be known. Historians think that most probably they were killed by Indians. But not so those that had dropped, footsore and exhausted, or strayed off on the long trek up through Mexico. These increased so rapidly, sometimes doubling their number every two years, that twenty-five years later Francisco de Ibarra reported he saw thousands running wild in the province of Sinaloa. Thirty years after that, one land-holder in the province of Jalisco was branding thirty thousand calves a year. Vast herds also grazed throughout Durango and Chihuahua. Although some were killed for meat, thousands were slaughtered just for their hides and tallow, or hard fat. The meat was left to rot on the carcasses. Yet even this killing made small inroads on the number of cattle infesting the thickets, prairies, and river bottoms.

The slaughtering was called a *matanza,* and was a time of great excitement and activity. First, the mounted *vaqueros* rounded up the cattle in a wild, noisy melee of riders, animals, shouting, spinning ropes, creaking saddle leather, and flying dirt and dung. They lanced the stock, or cut their throats. Indian laborers tended to the skinning and stretching of the hides. They rendered out the tallow and packed it into rawhide bags, and cut the flesh into strips for drying in the hot sun. Because the bloody hides, raw meat, and stinking offal drew myriad flies, buzzards, coyotes, and bears to the scene, the *vaqueros* spent many sleepless nights. At one *matanza*, they killed forty bears in one night!

The hides and tallow were hauled on horseback, or in horse-drawn carts to the east coast of Mexico, and then by ships to Spain. The profit resulting from the sale of these products was used to buy provisions for the settlers in the new land—kettles, knives, cloth, and other manufactured articles impossible to obtain in the New World. When word spread throughout Spain that there was both land and cattle for the taking in New Spain, more Spaniards migrated and founded haciendas. Small wonder! They need only take up unclaimed land, then hire a few native riders and laborers to build adobe ranch buildings, plant corn, and round up a herd. The thorny thickets and lush pastures were swarming with cattle. Of course, they were wild, spooky creatures who raced away whenever they got scent of man. During the day they hid out in the brush, and came out for feed and water only at night. They were extremely dangerous, difficult to rope and brand, and seldom became entirely gentled. But they were there for the taking, thousands upon thousands of them.

By this time Florida also was host to Spanish cattle, in the area of St. Augustine. Soon a sturdy fort was constructed there. Neighboring ranches also appeared, with arrangements to sell their beef to the military establishment. A thin trail through swamp, palmetto, and scrub pine across Florida connected the east coast fort with the west coast settlement at Tallahassee, then called San Luis. Some cattle may have been trailed to the west coast of Florida, but if so, they were slaughtered, and not kept for seed, or breeding stock.

In 1598 the Mexican-born Spanish explorer, Juan de Oñate, set out from Zacatecas, Mexico with a company of priests, laborers, and four hundred soldiers, one hundred and thirty of whom brought their families. There was the usual noisy conglomeration of sheep, swine, chickens, and horses, and seven thousand cattle. Oñate crossed the Rio Grande river, and founded a colony named San Juan, in north-central New Mexico. Undoubtedly a good number of these cattle strayed from the unfenced pastures, and gave rise to wild herds that made their home in the brush. Preyed upon by cougars, bears, and Indians, both the wild and the tame mission cattle fared poorly.

Trailing a herd through the wilderness was grueling work. The stock was ornery. The steers poked along, or drifted off the path, or tried to hide in the dagger-spiked brush. They bawled by the hour. A leaf spinning in front of them, a rattlesnake's vicious thrust, a bolt of lightning, any sudden noise or movement could bring on a wild run. At night they were prey to bears, wolves, and jaguars. The men riding with them suffered bone-deep fatigue and saddle sores, and put as many as twenty hours a day in the saddle. Yet from these earliest drives in America, the pattern of hardship and danger would never vary as long as the four-legged brutes moved on their own power from one part of the country to the other.

In 1685 still another herd of cattle brought to the New World fared poorly. That year the French explorer, René Robert Cavalier, Sieur de la Salle, sailed to the West Indies. He took with him Spanish cattle, swine, and chickens, and then charted his course for the mouth of the great river he had explored earlier, the Mississippi. But LaSalle overshot his mark in a storm, and landed his expedition further west on the coast of Matagorda Bay. Most of his livestock was eaten by his hungry men, and before long the fort he had erected was overrun with Indians.

When the Spanish authorities in Mexico learned that a French force had landed in territory claimed by Spain, they dispatched

Captain Alonso de León, Governor of Coahuila province, with soldiers, priests, laborers, cattle, horses, and supplies to found missions north of the Rio Grande river and along the coast. They called this region Texas, a word believed to be derived from an Indian word, *Texia*, which applied to a confederacy of Indian tribes occupying the eastern portion of the region. The Spanish form of the word was *Tejas*, and meant "allies" or "friends."

Thus it was that in 1690 Captain de León, along with Father Damian Massanet, founded two missions in Texas: the Mission San Francisco de los Tejas, near modern Nacogdoches, and the Mission Santa Maria on the Neches River, close by Louisiana Territory. It is said that the Captain left a bull and cow, and stallion and mare at every river crossing between the Rio Grande and Louisiana. Then at the missions, the remaining cattle were turned out to graze, and increase. The presence of the missions was supposed to make it clear to the French that Spain meant to control Texas.

The next year Domingo Teran los Rios was named Governor of Texas. He marched north with the usual complement of men and livestock. However the Indians—Apaches, Lipans, and Comanches—were so troublesome that within two years the governor was forced to withdraw to Mexico. He left the cattle behind, and before long they were running wild.

At that time there were two distinct breeds of Spanish cattle: the Moorish cattle, which were black, brave, and troublesome, and the Castilian cattle, which were brown, smaller, and easier to herd. In Spain, Mexico, and Texas, the two breeds were kept separated. But after the Spaniards withdrew from Texas, and left the cattle to wander aimlessly, the two breeds intermingled. As the years passed, the new animals, called Texas cattle, became formidable: they were large, mixed in color with a white, brown or yellow stripe running from the back of the neck to the tail. They possessed long horns, were fleet footed, very mean, and difficult to catch. They increased by the thousands, and moving from their original pastures, spread north and west as far as the Red River and the Brazos River country.

Undaunted by earlier failures to establish permanent missions, Captain Domingo Ramon ventured into Texas with more than a thousand cattle, sheep, and goats. The missions he started, and others near modern San Antonio, managed to gain a firm foothold. They, too, became well stocked with cattle. The first instances of cattle rustling developed about 1750 when the Indians began stealing domesticated cattle and driving them to the markets in Louisiana. But in spite of this, by the 1770's a mission near present-day Goliad, Texas boasted forty thousand head of cattle, and another west of San Antonio claimed ten thousand branded and twenty thousand unbranded wild cattle called *cimarrones*.

By the 1790's the Spaniards had extended their line of missions as far west as southern New Mexico and present-day Tucson, Arizona. Here, too, more cattle and sheep were brought in, but the Apaches killed off most of the cattle.

Since money was not yet used for trade, men conducted their business by bartering live cattle, or the meat, hides, and tallow. A man's worth was governed by the number of cattle he had under his own brand. Even the joyful fiestas were geared to cattle, as the wildest bulls were roped and brought in for riding and roping contests. However, there were no bull fights then, as there were later in Mexico.

Ranching was the single and largest activity in Texas. There were ranches on both sides of the Rio Grande river from modern Laredo downstream to its mouth. Wild cattle were found from the Rio Grande on the south to the Red River on the north, from Louisiana on the east to the lonely breaks of the Brazos River on the west. All this had come about in the less than three hundred years that had passed since the Spaniards first brought cattle to Mexico.

But change was in the air. In 1800 the first of a number of settlers from American territory on the north began to filter into Texas. They brought a few head of cattle with them, far different animals than the wily, wild Texas stock. The newly-arrived Americans were amazed to find Texas overrun with cattle. In turn, the Texans wondered where these poor, new shorthorned specimens had come from, and how they had reached Texas from the north.

But that was another story, one that began when the first cattle were brought to the Atlantic seaboard.

2

Colonial Cattle

Thirteen Colonies and Louisiana

Sunshine dappled the water the morning the *Susan Constant* hove to off the shore of present-day Virginia, in 1607. Soon small boats pulled for shore, bringing English families to found a new settlement called Jamestown. But people and their belongings were not the only things leaving the sturdy little vessel after its perilous journey across the Atlantic. A few head of cattle, sheep, swine, and horses were soon foundering in the shallows, and taking their first steps onto the New World. The cattle were probably gentle Devons, their red coats a cheerful note on the somber, forested shore.

The dark woods lightened as axes bit into the hard wood. Logs crashed, and a triangular blockhouse and several dwellings took shape. These first buildings were destroyed by fire in 1608, and immediately rebuilt. By 1609 the colony boasted another block-house, some fifty wooden structures, a chapel and storehouse, all surrounded by a palisade with a fort at the neck. The small herd grazed outside the stockade during the day, but was driven inside at night. But then famine almost wiped out the struggling colony, and all the livestock was eaten, even the horses.

In 1611 Sir Thomas Dale brought more colonists and livestock to

Virginia. Realizing that the animals were absolutely necessary to the future welfare of the people, he ordered that "no man shall dare to kill or destroy any without leave." So before too long the colonists had over two hundred cattle, and as many goats and hogs, and some horses. In 1619 two more ships left England for America, bringing still more people and 102 head of cattle. This stock did very well, and numbered from two to five thousand head by 1627. Six years later Virginia was able to send cattle to the struggling colonists in Massachusetts and Connecticut.

As the Jamestown settlement gained a firm hold in the New World, the cultivation of tobacco was introduced. Large farms, called plantations, were established to the east and west along the James River, and even as far as the York and Potomac rivers, and the east shore of Chesapeake Bay. And everywhere the colonists sought new land in the wilderness, they brought one or more head of cattle with them. But there were no cattle trailed over long distances. Wherever possible, the newcomers moved about on the rivers, using simple rafts to transport their household goods and livestock. The roads between the settlements were little more than paths through the woods.

The pioneers needed cattle badly. They were as dependent on them for food and hides as the Indians were on deer and buffalo. From a cow's milk and the cheese and butter made from it, families enjoyed health-giving food. Oxen helped pull their heavy wagons and plows. The meat was nutritious, the fat useful for cooking, soap-making, and candles. Even the intestines, turned inside out and cleaned, were used for sausage cases. The horns were carved into spoons, cups, hair ornaments, and powder horns. The hides, raw or tanned in supple leather, were used in many ways: to shield the door of a dugout or a window opening or floor; to cover wagon bows,

stools, cradles, buckets, dough pans, and trunks; to fashion in moccasins and shoes, leggings, shirts, shot pouches, and bed covers; as hobbles for livestock; and for lariats and harnesses and ropes; yes, even for burial wrappings, if a blanket or coffin was not available. Practically everything was used except the "moo."

In November of 1620, the *Mayflower* brought the first English colonists to New England. Forty-one men and their families, numbering one hundred and two persons in all, landed at a point where a huge granite boulder stood at the water's edge. This has since become famed Plymouth Rock, and the town Plymouth, Massachusetts.

Those beginning years were ones of great hardship, but the little group managed to scratch a toehold in the wilderness. A Captain

Edward Winslow brought three heifers and a bull from England in
1624. Governor Bradford of Plymouth Colony referred to them in
his journal as "the first beginning of any cattle of that kind in the
land."

The Dutch settled New York in 1614, and in the next decade
brought over from their country large red-and-white and black-and-
white Danish bulls and cows. Dutch schooners, sailing into Massa-

chusetts Bay, had no difficulty in selling heifers and other livestock to the Puritans. In 1630 John Mason, founder of New Hampshire, brought a group of Danes to grassy acres along the Piscataqua River. He also imported large, yellow Danish cattle to do the heavy hauling in his lumber and sawmill operations.

These early cattle had to scrounge for something to eat, because at this time there was no clover, or timothy, or bluegrass in the New World. The cattle ate "browse" and "swamp grass," broom straw, and rye. They did reasonably well nine months of the year, but really suffered for lack of good feed in the winter. Then, luckily, seeds from hay stored aboard an English vessel wafted ashore. These took root in the virgin soil, and soon sprouted vigorously into white clover and bluegrass. When this hay ripened, the farmers cut and stacked it, and thus had forage for their cattle during the winter.

Then on June 12, 1630 some nine hundred men, women, and children settled at Mishawum, later called Charleston. However, a lack of adequate fresh water forced them to move across to a peninsula known to the Indians as Shawmut. But the first settler there, William Blackstone, called it Trimountaine, because of a three-peaked hill nearby. Since many of the new arrivals had come from Boston, in Lincolnshire, England, it was not surprising that the new location was soon renamed Boston. This Massachusetts Bay Colony was headed by an unusually able man named John Winthrop. The new settlers brought a small herd of red-coated Devon cattle along, as well as horses, swine, and goats. More and more ships brought people and cattle to America, and all seemed to do well in and around Boston.

The town soon outstripped her neighbors in population and wealth. Her people were industriously occupied with farming, fishing, shipbuilding, shoe and boot making, and trading with other colonies, the West Indies, and England. Perhaps the hides first used in shoe making were imported, but before long the local supply could meet the needs of the leather manufacturers.

Boston's cattle were pastured on the Boston Common, laid out in 1634 as a combination military parade ground and common pasture. On its fifty acres of grass and trees, many cattle fed under the care of a man hired by the town to drive the livestock to the Common, watch over them, and return them to their pens each night. This practice was to continue for two centuries. No person was permitted to pasture more than one cow or four sheep there, and tickets were issued to those who used the Common. Each cow was branded and ear-marked, and these marks were registered with the town officials. Those without tickets had to take their livestock elsewhere. The cattle were not allowed to stray over the town and its outlying fields until after the fall harvest. Then the fences were lowered, or gates opened, and the livestock foraged all winter amidst the stubble.

In the 1670's the need for more land for pasturage was the strong reason behind the founding of many settlements in Massachusetts, Connecticut, Rhode Island, New Hampshire, and Vermont. Driving cattle from place to place, or from farm to market in this early colonial period was almost entirely an individual effort. With the help of a young son or two, or a neighbor's boy, the owner poked his cattle over meadows and through dark woods, often along age-old Indian paths. At night he slept out with his stock, and completed their sale by himself.

As the years passed, farmers found it necessary to make longer drives to market, as much as one hundred miles or more. By 1655 cattle were being driven from Springfield to Boston. An early account states that "almost as soon as there were highways to the north and west, they were filled in their season with droves of cattle that were pastured on the hills of New Hampshire or the remote areas later known as Vermont. Year after year the business of the drovers increased. Brighton became one of the great cattle marts of the country, and salt beef became an important article of export from Boston."

Meantime Tidewater, Virginia, close to the coast and along the rivers that emptied into the Atlantic Ocean, drew more and more settlers. Many did not have the means to establish plantations and buy seed for large crops. They pushed farther west with a few head of cattle into the lush Shenandoah Valley, and made stock raising their principal activity. They spread throughout the Piedmont, the rich land between the coast and the Blue Ridge mountains.

Within fifty years there were herds of four and five hundred cattle supplying the frontier posts of that region, as well as the markets in the larger cities like Richmond and Raleigh. In spite of this mushrooming activity, there is no record of there being a major, much-used cattle trail from the interior to the coast. Apparently each stockman drove his own herd over his own route to the nearest market.

As still more people poured into the frontier, the families reached out southward, into Carolina. They sought land and better pasturage for their stock. Here the shorthorned cattle down from Virginia met the longhorned Spanish cattle that had drifted up from Florida and Georgia. By the 1850's, great beef herds were being driven from this region as far north as Baltimore, Charleston, Norfolk, and even Philadelphia. One early account stated it was "not an uncommon thing to see one man master of from 300 to 1,200, and even 2,000 bulls, oxen and young cattle."

In 1773, James Oglethorpe founded Georgia as a refuge for debtors and persecuted Protestants. The newcomers to the land

lying between the Savannah and Ogeechee rivers found themselves in possession of one of the finest cattle ranges in the south. Their animals ranged there almost free of flies and leeches, and "water rot" and "scald" diseases that afflicted cattle in southernmost and coastal Georgia and northern Florida. These back-country Georgians soon were dubbed "Georgia crackers" because of the noises they made with their whips when driving stock to market. Cattle did so well that during the Revolution, many herds were driven north to supply the soldiers of the Revolutionary Army.

Cattle raising in colonial America stretched from New Hampshire on the north to Georgia on the south, in an almost continuous line; in the New England foothills of the Berkshire and White mountains; in New York around Albany and the Mohawk Valley; in Pennsylvania surrounding Philadelphia, dropping down through Virginia's Shenandoah Valley, the Carolinas, and the Georgia Piedmont.

In contrast, the New England coastal colonies were busy with fishing and lumbering; the middle colonies with trading; the South with plantations producing rice, tobacco, cotton, and indigo. Unlike the Texans, who at this date marketed cattle only for the hides and tallow, the Atlantic colonies' stockmen raised animals suitable for three purposes: for plowing and hauling, for milking, and for meat. And unlike those early Texans, they profited more from their cattle, bought more manufactured goods, and gradually bettered their standard of living.

Although not part of the original thirteen colonies, Lousiana and Mississippi also possessed cattle at this time. They were first introduced by a Frenchman named Sieur d'Iberville, who brought cattle from France to Biloxi, Mississippi in 1699. The gentle cattle did well, and in time their offspring were trailed from one French outpost to another as far north as St. Louis, and even up the Wabash, Wisconsin, and Illinois rivers.

Cattle flourished in Louisiana after the Acadians, French settlers from Nova Scotia, settled there in 1765. Each family strived to possess five cows with calves, and a bull. Within twenty-five years, over three hundred thousand French cattle were said to be feeding on the grass that grew back high on a horse. Many of these cattle, as well as a lesser number from the easternmost-Texas settlements, supplied the bustling meat and hide market in New Orleans, and were flat-boated up the Mississippi as white men reached farther and farther up the great river.

In the 1670's a new kind of businessman appeared on the scene. Though roughly dressed in homespun, and accustomed to sleeping and eating out of doors, he immediately was welcomed by the farmers. This was the cattle trader. He was a man who moved through the country, buying cattle right at the farmer's pasture gate. He took over the onerous task of moving the purchased cattle to slaughter houses. When one or two men were successful at this, others entered the business. They smooth-talked the farmers, and drove as hard bargains as they could. Often they dickered a long day before buying a few head. If they were lucky, they got a home-cooked meal and an invitation to spread their blankets in the barn at night, as part of the bargaining. As soon as the sale was completed, the trader turned the cattle over to his helper, who tended the growing herd while the trader dickered elsewhere for more cattle. Finally, when from one to five hundred head had been purchased, trader and helper "drove" the herd to the nearest slaughterhouse.

In colonial times, there was only one trail that was as widely known as it was widely used. It was north, in Massachusetts. In moving their cattle from west to east in the colony, drovers got in the habit of converging along the banks of the Blackstone River, near present-day Worcester. From there they followed the same cowpath eastward past Hopkinton and Dedham, on into Boston. As hundreds of barnyard cattle beat down this trail, it became known as the Bay State Cow Path.

There were no exciting stampedes described in early accounts of traffic on this old thoroughfare. No wild cattle towns sprung up to serve the cattlemen, similar to Abilene and Dodge City, Kansas in a later day. There were no cowboys on the Cow Path; no chuck-wagons, no talk flavored with Spanish words, as in Texas. Yet the Bay State Cow Path wove a strong thread in the fabric of New England's economy.

One of the unheralded stories of the American Revolution is that of the farmers and traders who braved Loyalist opposition and moved beef and farm products over the Cow Path to Army supply headquarters. Many remained, with older sons, to enlist in the Army and fight for freedom. And by the time the survivors returned to their farms, New England was almost stripped of cattle.

Because these farmers needed a quick cash crop, they plowed up their pastures and planted grains, instead of rebuilding their herds. But in time they sent to England, Scotland, Holland, and Denmark for more breeding stock. Even when these cattle began producing marketable herds, traffic remained pokey on the old Cow Path. Portions of it eventually were supplanted by improved post roads over which stagecoaches and freight wagons rattled between Boston, Springfield, New Haven, and other towns.

After steamboats appeared on major rivers, cattle could be moved easier and quicker to market that way. Still some drovers and traders clung to the Cow Path because there were no toll charges, the grass was free, and if not pushed, cattle actually gained weight on the way to market.

For over a hundred years the venerable Bay State Cow Path served the hub of a new nation. Today its existence is largely forgotten, and nowhere is there a marker to note its place in colonial history.

3

Wilderness Trails

Pennsylvania to Kentucky and Ohio

Not all the early settlers on the Atlantic coast were from England. Unbeknownst to the Jamestown settlers, Henry Hudson, sailing for the Dutch East India Company, entered Delaware Bay in 1609. Dutch traders followed not long afterward, and named a beautiful stream the Schuylkill River. But the first Europeans to make a real settlement in what is now Pennsylvania were Swedes. In 1638 they brought barnyard cattle with them to their new settlement close to the present boundaries of Philadelphia. Still more cattle came when a second company took up land near present-day Wilmington, Delaware, in 1643. But both were taken over by the Dutch, and still later by the English. All were skilled, diligent farmers who produced good crops, and their cattle flourished.

In 1681 William Penn became the proprietor and governor of the new province of Pennsylvania. A deeply religious man, Penn planned to establish a colony of Quakers where men and women might live in peace, free of persecution. But he was also a very practical man, and sent men ahead of him to lay out the site for a new town. He chose its name, Philadelphia, from a Greek word meaning brotherly love.

In the late summer of 1682, several shiploads of emigrants left for the new colony. These earliest arrivals had to dig caves to shelter their families. Their cattle foraged on good grass. By 1685 about 2,500 people were living in Philadelphia in homes built of wood, stone, and brick. By early 1700 the streets were no longer meandering cowpaths. Though the center cartway was unpaved and full of mudholes, there were brick sidewalks for the people to trod. Behind most homes were small barns to house the family cows and calves. Young boys had the chore of driving them to and from the pastures.

Like Boston, Philadelphia became one of the major cities in the colonial times. Her people ate well. Usually there was plenty of meat on the table: venison, goose, wild turkey, bear, pork, and some beef. But as more people poured in, there was less and less wild game. The city folk began to need more beef, and could pay a fair price for it. So some Quakers and Swedish farmers who had taken land up and down the Schuylkill, Potomac, and adjoining rivers, began raising beef solely for market. Their places were not called ranches, or even farms. They were called cow-pens.

A cow-pen usually consisted of one hundred acres enclosed by high woods, and divided into three sections. One contained a good-sized house, barn, chicken house, and other sheds. A second was devoted to the corn patch and family vegetable garden. The third was left in pasture. The cattle fended for themselves in the neighboring fields and woods, and were half wild. In time the herds built up to five hundred or a thousand head. Every March the cow-pen master and his men rounded up the cows and their new calves, put them in the fenced pasture, and branded and marked the calves. In September they were turned out again to find their own browse in the woods. In October the fat steers and dry cows were driven to the market at Philadelphia.

In 1710 a large number of Germans came to Pennsylvania. For religious reasons they did not want to live alongside the Quakers, so they bought good farm land farther westward. The Quakers didn't mind. They liked the idea of having other settlers between them and the Indians! Within ten years there were German farms, villages, and cattle almost all the way to the Susquehanna River. These people traded for bulls and cows among each other, but often had to buy some of the English cattle brought over by the Quakers. Before long there was an intermingling of English, Dutch, German, and Swedish cattle.

The Scotch-Irish came about that same time, looking for cheap or free land. They pushed deeper into the great plateau that stretched between the Appalachians and the Atlantic. They were a feisty, independent people, and not very good farmers or stockmen. But they did take to the woods, and carried the line of habitation further and further west.

The Scotch-Irish raised large families. When their children married, they left home and took up land beyond their parents' settlements. If they were very fortunate, these young couples might possess a quilt or two, a rifle, a kettle and skillet, an axe, a little corn seed and a scraggly cow. Man and wife worked together to hack a clearing in the forest, raise a cabin with their neighbor's help, and plant corn. They lived on bear meat and venison, slept on flea-ridden bear robes, tanned their own leather for shirts and shoes, and scratched a living out of the wilderness. They were rough and dirty, and could not read or write. When neighbors got too close, they moved deeper into the woods. The English and Dutch settlers who came after them possessed money and tools enough to establish a proper farm with a barn, outbuildings, cornfield, and hay meadow, and stock it with good livestock.

All this time there were no lengthy overland trails over which cattle moved to eastern markets. Most cattle were raised and marketed within a small area. Few were sold for actual money, because most were exchanged for grain, tools, and services.

Many householders made their own leather. This was a smelly, unpleasant task. First the hair had to be removed by soaking the hide in a vat containing water and wood ashes. Then it was washed, liberally sprinkled with chips of oak and hemlock bark, and placed in a trough filled with water. Tannic acid leached from the bark chips. As the hide soaked in this solution, for as long as six months, it became tanned. Then it was removed, washed again, oiled with bear oil, and worked to a softness by being rubbed and scraped with the dull edge of a knife.

As late as 1750, even the settlements farthest from the coast stopped short of the high slopes of the Appalachian Mountains. The ridges and slopes on the west side of the range were too steep, too densely timbered, and too overrun with unfriendly Indians to tempt most people to move there. But the French and Indian War changed that. In 1775 General Braddock had a road cut from Fort Cumberland in Maryland almost to the Ohio River. Three years later there was a trail cleared from Harrisburg almost to present-day Pittsburgh.

After the defeated French withdrew from the region, the soldiers who had fought in the war and had seen this unclaimed land began to move west. They brought cattle with them. One group penetrated the southern Appalachians and settled about the Watauga River, in extreme eastern Tennessee. Watauga became the jumping off place for Kentucky, long rumored as a region of great beauty, tall trees, rich soil, and thick grass.

Daniel Boone, accompanied by forty coonskin-capped, buckskin-clad frontiersmen, blazed a road through Cumberland Gap. Then he continued along an ancient buffalo trail to a place near present-day Lexington, Kentucky where he and his men built a fort with four blockhouses. As soon as word seeped throughout the East that the way to "Caintuck" was now open, thanks to Boone's Trace, settlers began to pour in. Although much blood was shed in skirmishes with the Indians, the settlers kept on coming. The road was barely passable in spots. Many turnouts around bog holes and big trees and rocks gave it twistings and turnings. But the settlers led their ox-drawn wagons and poked their milk cows all the way to Kentucky.

After the War of Independence ended in 1781, some six thousand people moved into Kentucky. Many came with their belongings and livestock by flatboat down the Ohio. In one seven month period, 177 boats dubbed Noah's Arks, carried 1,300 horses, hundreds of sheep and hogs and poultry, and 766 cattle to Kentucky. In the next year over 900 boats came downriver with emigrant families, much livestock, and over 2,500 cattle. Within a few years the new farms were producing excellent crops, and there were more cattle than the people could use.

"If only we had a market where we could sell the critters," the farmers complained to one another. The countryside seemed overrun with cattle.

"Richmond is the closest place, but it's nigh onto six hundred miles away," one man mentioned.

"It would take two months to get there," another added.

"And another two months gettin' back."

But they really had no choice, if they wanted to sell their surplus cattle. Thus out of necessity, an era of colorful long drives began.

The first land route used was Boone's Wilderness Road. The general route stretched from central Kentucky, over Cumberland Gap, through the Blue Ridge Mountains, and on into Richmond. The first drive probably took place in 1802. It was so successful a venture that more farmers took to the trail. Soon it became known as the Wilderness Trail, and no trail was ever more appropriately named. For twenty years thousands of cattle made the long, strenuous drive through dark woods, over rocky outcroppings and across marshy ground. Trailing a herd through the mountainous wilderness was grueling work.

Although Kentucky was a favored land, settlers pushed on into Ohio, and then Indiana and Illinois. There they found the lush prairie grass and sweet water put flesh on their animals. By 1822 the prairie stretches of the frontier were vast, unfenced feeder lots. As soon as a surplus developed, cattle men looked east for a market.

Roads were opened to New York as well as through Pennsylvania. One heavily used road went from Columbus, Ohio northwest to Dunkirk and Buffalo, along the Erie Canal to Utica and Albany, and south into New York City. Another started at Mount Vernon, Ohio and went due east to Pittsburgh. Still another started at Columbus or Zanesville, crossed three mountain ranges—the Tuscarora, Kittatinny, and Blue mountains—and then strung out to Harrisburg or Baltimore. With its many side roads or feeders, it became known as the Three Mountain Trail.

Still, there was no denying the fact: getting cattle to market was a long, long, tedious, even dangerous business. Farmers were reluctant to leave their wives and children four months of the year in order to sell five or ten or twenty head. The men were needed at home to attend to the heavier farm chores. Yet all possessed surplus cattle, and needed to sell them in order to have some cash to buy other goods. So, two new things developed. Both would give impetus to the business of driving cattle in the east.

First, buyers who lived in New York, Philadelphia, and Baltimore began riding in gigs as far west as Harrisburg and Pittsburgh. There they intercepted the herds, and after much haggling over price, bought them on the spot. The farmers could pocket the cash and return home, because the buyers used their own crews of drovers to drive the livestock the remaining distance to the slaughterhouses in the big cities.

These buyers were called speculators, because they speculated, or gambled that they would receive a higher price at the slaughterhouse than they had paid the farmers for their stock. Not all the speculators were honest. Many indulged in a very unscrupulous practice. They instructed their drovers to let the cattle have plenty of salt the day before they reached the market. Then the thirsty cattle were allowed to drink their fill of water. This way each animal put on many extra pounds temporarily, and weighing more, brought a higher price. This practice brought a new term into our language, that of "watered stock," meaning an article or investment far above its true value.

Second, men like John Murray made an actual business of cattle droving. This had not been done before. In 1828, Murray shaped up a herd in Lake County, Ohio. Some of the cattle were his own, but others he bought from neighbors. Very little cash changed hands at this time. The farmers and Murray agreed on a price that would be paid for the cattle *after* Murray returned from selling them in the east. There was always much hemming and hawing and chewing tobacco before the price was agreed upon. It had to be high enough to satisfy the farmer, but low enough so Murray could sell at a still higher price in the east, and thus make a profit for his efforts.

After he had gathered about three hundred head, Murray and his sons road-branded them. A road brand was a cover brand for cattle obtained from numerous owners but traveling under single ownership. It established the drover's claim to the herd in case of theft, stampede or other accidents on the road.

After the branding, Murray and his sons turned the cattle onto the trail. Going over the mountains, the road was very rocky and often not more than twenty feet wide. Occasionally an animal plunged down the steep banks to its death, but most arrived safely at the market in Pennsylvania. Murray probably paid about fifteen to twenty dollars a head for his cattle, and sold them for from thirty to forty dollars a head. At any rate, he made enough money on this first risky venture to warrant trying it again, and again, all told for thirty years! But as soon as he had proved that cattle droving could be a profitable *business,* not a haphazard gamble, quite a few other men began moving large herds to the east.

The trails used by these men were referred to as "drove roads," and had many names. Farmers whose lands adjoined or crossed the roads began offering lodging, meals, and corn or pasture for the cattle. During the summer so many drovers moved along the trails that a person, a mile or more away, could tell of the passing stock because of the long lines of dust rising in the air. In the spring the clay pikes, as some roads were called, were all but impassable in deep mud. The cattle, walking two abreast as was their custom, wore deep trenches in the roads. When these dried, they made the way impossible for wagons and carriages.

There were no cowboys or top hands, as there were later on the

trail up from Texas. The crew consisted of a boss who rode horse-back, his saddle bags containing an extra shirt and pair of socks for himself and his men. Behind his saddle was a roll of extra garments which the men donned if the weather was rainy. The boss carried a long black whip which he cracked over the cattle's heads to keep them moving and in line. These whips had linen strips on their tips

that crackled like rifle fire. Hearing a drove go through the woods, an unsuspecting person might think a band of hunters was passing.

Another man on horseback had the job of keeping the forward part of the line in order, and getting the herd past intersecting roads. He rode out front with the lead animal, with a rope attached to its horns. At the rear, another man armed with a whip kept the laggards from dropping back. At noon time the herd halted, rested, and grazed. The men made coffee and chewed cold meat and biscuit. After a hasty bite, the boss went on ahead to make arrangements for pasture and lodging.

For their hard work, the drovers were paid fifteen dollars a month and their food while on the trail. Lodging usually turned out to be a blanket or straw pallet spread on the floor of a tavern "common room," one large enough to accommodate thirty men. For fifty cents extra, the herd owner could stretch out on a hard bunk covered with a dirty sack of hay. The food was as good as the landlord allowed, rough, plain, but filling. Every stopping place sold liquor, but for the most part there was only occasional trouble because of this. Some men were robbed after becoming intoxicated, and probably one or two were murdered.

The herds averaged from nine to twelve miles a day. It took from forty to fifty days to travel from Ohio to the markets in Pennsylvania. If a herd trampled down fences, or overran gardens, the drover had to pay for the damage. All told, possibly three million cattle were driven from Ohio to the eastern markets. Of course, these herds were not the only ones on the road. There was a constant parade of sheep and swine, and particularly horses and mules destined for the Pennsylvania coal mines. The dust never settled on the trail, and it is said that one herd followed on the heels of another.

Today, few people realize that the east as well as the west had its great cattle drives. There is no trace left of the interlocking maze of cattle trails that enabled frontier cattle to reach the markets of the Atlantic seaboard.

4

The Texas Road

Missouri to Texas; St. Louis to Dallas

While Americans were venturing as far west as Illinois and very slowly building small herds of cattle on the thick prairie grass, Frenchmen were opening up new country across the broad brown Mississippi River. The French had a line of communication between their settlements in Canada and Louisiana along the west bank of the river. These were mostly miserable log cabins set on mud flats near the water. They sheltered fearless hunters and trappers who traveled far, exploring the tributary streams in their quest for furs.

But not all these men traveled by water. Some pushed further west and south on an old well-worn Indian trail. It led into the cross-timber woodland and hills claimed by the powerful Osage Indians for their hunting grounds, and encompassed the area between St. Louis, eastern Kansas, present-day Oklahoma, and as far south as the Red River, the future Texas boundary. Shortly after the French came onto the scene, so many Osage streamed up through eastern Oklahoma and across Missouri to St. Louis to trade their furs, beeswax, and bear grease for kettles, cloth, and geegaws, that their trail became known as the Osage Trace.

In 1803 the United States purchased the Louisiana Territory from

France, and all this land became the property of the government. Almost immediately Americans rafted across the Mississippi and took up land along the Osage Trace. The few head of cattle they transported with their meager belongings were scrubby shorthorns. Some of these people were restless folk, who pushed ever southward. A number filtered into southeast Texas where the Spaniards and Mexicans had settled some two centuries earlier. Other Americans, mostly farmers, arrived after Moses Austin obtained permission from the Mexican government to settle three hundred families in Texas. Austin's son, Stephen, established the first permanent Anglo-American colony at San Felipe de Austin on the lower Brazos River, in December of 1821.

When accounts of this unoccupied fertile region overrun with cattle spread throughout the east, more land-hungry Americans emigrated to Texas. Thirty thousand arrived during the next fifteen years. They took up many acres mainly along the rivers between San Antonio and Nacogdoches. Being so remote from the seat of Spanish authority, they more or less governed themselves.

The Americans looked at the Texas cattle, and mistakenly thought they were native to Texas. The Spaniards and Mexicans gazed pityingly at the poor spindly cattle brought in by the newcomers. At first the wild Spanish cattle would have nothing to do with the shorthorns, perhaps because they bore the scent of man. But those that did not die of tick fever eventually wandered into the thickets, mingled with the wild ones, and in time were completely assimilated by them.

The American colonists hunted the wild cattle relentlessly for their meat and hides. They found them as flighty and watchful as turkeys, and very dangerous. They were far more difficult to shoot than the plentiful deer. Some of the men foolishly attempted to run

them down on horseback. Often a wild bull would turn with incredible swiftness and gore both horse and rider, with all going down in a heap together. Other times, a hapless hunter found himself high-tailing it for the nearest tree, an enraged bull snorting at his heels.

To build a herd, a man needed only a rope and a branding iron—and the courage to use both. The wild cattle did not run in herds. A few cows and calves could be found together, but the bulls were almost always alone. One way to round them up was to drive the wild cattle out of the thickets and keep them on the move two or three days until they were so worn out that they could be managed in small bunches. Another way was to rope the wild stock and hog-tie them to trees until they became half-way gentle. Still another was to drive a decoy of domesticated cattle into the brush, and then drive out the tame and wild ones together. Sometimes a rider came up behind a cow or bull, and wrapped its tail around the saddle horn; then the rider spurred his horse and jerked the captured animal off the ground so its feet could be tied together. It remained hobbled until gentled. Other times cattle were trapped near water holes or salt licks, and driven into pens where the wild ones were yoked to tame oxen. The quickest, but by no means the safest, way to build a herd was to separate wild calves from the cows and put them in fenced pastures.

As the English-speaking Texans became more skilled at roping, riding, and trailing cattle, they rivaled the Mexican *vaqueros*. They began to call themselves cowboys, instead of stock boys or herders. They also set the pattern for a way of life that would spread throughout the West. They trained so-called "cutting horses," fast mounts taught to cut a certain animal out of a herd. Then, as the settlers acquired more and more cattle and put them out to graze on the free grass, they found it necessary for neighbor to band with neighbor in the late spring to round up the cows with calves who had strayed into the brush.

To do this, a dozen men would gather, each with from one to three horses, blankets, and some sugar, salt, coffee, and bread. (They would kill deer or unbranded cattle for meat.) They were equipped with lassos, six-shooters and bowie knives. They never knew when they might encounter a ferocious bull. The owners ranged over a wide portion of the country, and drove the strays into one large herd. Then they cut out the cattle belonging to each other, marked, branded, and altered the calves, and divided any unbranded cattle among themselves.

The term "maverick" cropped up at this time. In 1845 a Texas lawyer named Samuel A. Maverick accepted four hundred cattle as payment of a debt owed him. He was not a cattleman and did not even have his herd branded. The animals roamed on Matagorda Island off the Texas coast until 1853, when Maverick had them moved up the San Antonio River, and sold them. The other cattlemen in the region branded their stock, so whenever they saw an unbranded stray, they usually said, "That's Maverick's." Later they said, "That's a Maverick." In time the term applied to any unbranded stray, and even today it is used to describe a person or animal that is a loner.

After the spring roundup, each rancher drove his cattle home. There, most were turned out to graze, while others were driven to the nearest market, and slaughtered for hides and tallow.

There was a strong market for tallow. In those days the tallow "dip" or candle furnished light. Housewives dipped their own candles, but already, mostly in the east and abroad, manufacturers made candles by machinery. The hides sold for harnesses, shoes, and other articles. The hoofs and horns were bought by glue manufacturers. Small firms sold pickled beef by the barrel, but fresh beef spoiled too quickly to be sold in any but markets close to a slaughterhouse. Since most of a cow or beef could be used except the meat, only the skinned carcasses were left to rot in the sun, and were devoured by coyotes, buzzards, and wolves.

Gradually those who settled south of the Red River brought large herds under control. In the first book published about Texas in English, Mary Austin Holley described the principal occupation as "farming and raising black cattle." Black cattle and linebacks— those with a light stripe from neck to tail—still predominated. Some were splotched underneath, and called "yellow bellies." There was always a mixture of red, brown, and even blue animals. No one has described these cattle better than J. Frank Dobie in his book *The Longhorns.* He wrote they were "tall, bony coarse-haired, flat-sided, thin-flanked, some of them grotesquely narrow-hipped, some with bodies so long that their backs swayed, big ears carved into outlandish designs, dewlaps hanging and swinging in rhythm with their energetic steps, their motley colored sides as bold with brands as a relief map of the Grand Canyon—mightily antlered, wild-eyed . . . But however they appeared, with their steel hoofs, their long legs, their stag-like muscles, their thick skins, their powerful horns, they could walk the roughest ground, cross the widest deserts, climb the highest mountains, swim the widest rivers, fight off the fiercest bands of wolves, endure cold, hunger, thirst and punishment as few beasts of the earth have ever shown themselves capable of enduring. On the prairies they could run like antelopes; in the thickets of thorn and tangle they could break their way with the agility of panthers."

Many decades of fending for themselves, of warding off screwworm flies, ticks, and crippling heel flies, wolves, Indian hunters, drouth, and blizzards had made the cattle very self-reliant. They were restless animals, constantly snuffing the air and on the lookout for danger. Unlike plodding domestic stock, they moved with a light elastic step. They formed the backbone of the economy which enabled the Texas-American colonists to survive and prosper in a harsh land.

Meantime, while the new Texans were becoming established, there was great pressure along the Atlantic seaboard and adjoining white settlements to remove all the Indians out of that vast area in the east, and re-settle them west of the Mississippi on government-owned land. These Indians possessed rich farmlands, particularly in Georgia, which white men coveted. Congress was prevailed upon to pass a shameful law which forced members of the so-called Five Civilized Tribes—the Cherokees, Choctaws, Creeks, Chickasaws, and Seminoles—to trade their lands in the south for unoccupied land in what became Oklahoma.

The Osage protested the intrusion of the five tribes on their hunting grounds, but could not back up their protests because by this time, 1829, their great tribal strength had been weakened by disease and warfare. The Osage were packed off to a reservation in eastern Kansas. The removal of the Five Civilized Tribes to this newly-formed Indian Territory took more than a decade to complete. It was accomplished only with much hardship and some bloodshed.

The Indians moved either by government-chartered boats up the Arkansas River, or on foot or horseback down the Osage Trace to their new homes in Oklahoma.

As more and more white settlers moved across the Mississippi, the southbound traffic on the Osage Trace increased. By 1835 it was the principal highway linking the midwest with Texas. Hundreds of families, with heavily-laden Conestoga wagons and livestock, moved south on it, and settled below the Red River in Texas. It was not unusual for the white emigrants' wagons to be backed up a mile, waiting for a primitive ferry to take them across the Arkansas River. Their cattle were swum across. As these families established themselves, they needed markets for their crops. So the traffic on the old Trace began to move in both directions as cattle, hides, cotton, wool, and mustangs, or wild horses, were sent north to St. Louis. Thus began, in this small and modest way, the movement of hundreds of thousands of bawling cattle northbound from Texas.

The distance from Dallas, then a dirty clutch of cabins, to St. Louis, was over six hundred miles. At the southern end, the cattle, mostly five- and six-year-old steers, were driven from as far south as Waco and Austin to Dallas. They continued north across the prairie to the Red River. The favorite fording was Rocky Bluff Crossing, near present-day Preston. A natural "chute" in the rocky bluff enabled the cattle to reach the river safely. Low banks on the north side made it easy for them to leave the water and enter Oklahoma. By the late 1830's there was a ferry, no more than a log raft, on which wagons could cross, but the cattle were always swum across. During low water stage, they could walk almost the entire river bed.

On the far side the cattle entered Oklahoma land settled by the Choctaw and trailed fifty miles to Boggy Depot, a settlement near Clear Boggy Creek. But the Indians whose lands lay astride the

Osage Trace found their fences knocked down and crops overrun by the cattle. They began demanding a beef or two in payment for these damages, or for the privilege of crossing their property.

One Choctaw, named Charles Leflore, had settled in the Limestone Hills. This was a difficult and tedious area to cross, unless the cattle were driven through a natural gap which afforded easier footing. Leflore put a fence and gate across the opening to Limestone Gap, and demanded a toll of ten cents a head. The drovers had no choice but to pay. Rather than permit a few members to enrich themselves by extracting such tolls, the Choctaw Tribal Council voted to charge fifty cents a head for cattle passing Choctaw-owned lands, and put this money into their general tribal fund.

Farther on up the road, the cattle crossed the Canadian River, and went through Creek country, where another fifty cent toll per head was extracted. The Osage Trace continued north to the Arkansas River, crossed it near the confluences of the Grand (Neosho) and Verdigris rivers, and strung out along the west bank of the Grand. After swinging past Fort Gibson, established in 1824, it entered country settled by Cherokee Indians, where the toll charge was seventy-five cents a head. The cattlemen were furious, but had to pay because the Indians had their own courts and laws, and could confiscate herds of those refusing to pay.

Fifteen miles south of the Kansas line, the cattle crossed to the east bank of the Grand, moved northeast up through Missouri to the Missouri River, and then trailed down the riverside wagon road to St. Louis. Even in the early days, the Osage Trace was wide enough to accommodate Conestoga wagons, military vehicles, freight wagons laden with buffalo robes and furs, as well as northbound herds of cattle, Mexican mules, and mustang ponies.

The drives of eight- to ten-year-old mature steers weighing from one thousand to twelve hundred pounds usually started in June. Aside from crossing flood-swollen rivers, it moved at a leisurely pace, taking about two and a half months to reach the northern market. There were always young boys on the drive, boys who could stand twelve or more hours daily in the saddle, sleeping on the ground in wet or dry weather, and eating the monotonous diet of meat and coffee. The adventure so whetted their desires to ride north that the very real dangers brought about by floods, storms, and stampedes could not hold them back.

As the years passed, travelers forgot that this was an age-old Indian road. They dropped the name Osage Trace, and thereafter spoke of it as the Texas Road. A few called it the Beef Trail.

The thoroughfare was not the only thing to have a new name. By now men spoke not of Spanish cattle, or Texas cattle, but of Longhorns. And Longhorns they were—powerful, half-wild animals sporting polished horns that often measured three to six feet from tip to tip. No one can explain satisfactorily how or why the horns developed so out of proportion, particularly since the forebearers of these animals had short, spiked horns. But grow long they did, to give an unforgettable picture-word name to a pioneer breed of cattle.

After Fort Gibson was established in 1824, drovers did not have to go the long distance to St. Louis. The fort was the most important military post in Oklahoma. It was connected by improved roads with Fort Smith directly southeast in Arkansas, and Fort Scott northward on the Kansas-Missouri border. At the Three Forks, where the Arkansas, Grand, and Verdigris rivers came together near Fort Gibson, cattle buyers congregated to buy beef to supply the military posts. The cattlemen liked this, not only because they could dispose of their cattle earlier and return home, but because the government buyers paid in cash, a scarce frontier commodity.

Trailing cattle developed into such a profitable business that out-laws soon took note. Several banded together. They attacked the drovers and ran off their livestock. Small parties were helpless against them, but soon the drovers began to join together for protection.

"Waste no time palaverin' with 'em. Shoot first and make it count," the drovers advised each other. Whenever they were able to overpower the outlaws, they hung them from the nearest tree. In spite of this, hijacking cattle continued for all the years that cattle were trailed north.

In 1843 a new and thriving market opened for the Texas cattle. Thousands of emigrants, including many members of the Mormon faith, outfitted at Independence and Westport, Missouri, prepara-tory to setting out on the Oregon Trail for the Pacific Northwest, or Utah. The dust never settled over the cattle and horse markets in those two outfitting towns situated on the Missouri River. Thus many of the cattle reaching Oregon and Utah were Texas stock, but a greater number were shorthorns drawn from Iowa, Missouri, Wisconsin, and Illinois.

Regardless of their point of origin, these cattle were called "stockers," because they were used to stock new ranches and ranges out West.

Then, in 1849, still another market opened for Texas cattle men as thousands of Forty-Niners crossed the Texas Road on their way to the gold fields of California. So much has been written of the vast movement through Missouri and out over the Oregon and Overland trails, that the traffic on the more southerly route has been all but forgotten.

Many gold-seekers gathered at Fort Smith on the Arkansas-Oklahoma border and crossed the Arkansas River near Salina,

Oklahoma. This was an historic spot on the Texas Road, being the location of a very early fur post established by August Pierre Choteau near a large salt lick favored by the Osage Indians. The old post later was taken over by the government and became one of the major trading points along the Texas Road. So many people congregated there in 1849 that the government established a postoffice, and named it Saline.

While these companies of gold seekers laid over to organize for their long journey, others came down from the north on the Texas Road, crossed the Grand River nearby, and rendezvoused at North Fork Town. Then the two groups blazed a route across Oklahoma, the Texas Panhandle, New Mexico, and Arizona to California. Many of the wagons were drawn by oxen, and most families at least started out with a head or two of beef cattle and a milk cow.

In spite of the risks involved, several Texas cattlemen walked herds of a hundred head or more to California. In Texas their cattle were worth from five to fifteen dollars a head, but could bring from twenty-five to two hundred dollars a head if they reached a gold camp. Of course, on the way the cattle would have to survive heat, dust, alkali, stampedes, storms, parched grass, poisonous weeds, bad water, sore feet, and Apache raiders. Although the route became lined with the carcasses of dead animals, a surprising number eked through the perilous journey and arrived, thin, worn, and avid for good grass and sweet water. They competed in the market places with California cattle, descendants of those brought two centuries earlier by the Spaniards who had established a line of missions through the golden province.

Thus the Texas Road played an important part in funneling Texas cattle and many gold-seekers on the California Road.

After the gold rush petered out in the 1850's, cattle continued to move briskly along the Texas Road between Texas and the Missouri River. There seemed to be no lessening in the demand for cattle. Traders who bought and fattened herds on the Illinois prairie before marketing them at Chicago, or farther east, began appearing on the Texas Road. They went far into Texas to buy from white ranchers, and also took delivery of small bunches from Indian farmers in the Nations, where the five civilized tribes had settled. It was not unusual for herds purchased in Missouri to wend their way across the Mississippi on rafts, then move through Illinois, Indiana, Ohio, and Pennsylvania to eastern seaboard markets. The most spectacular drive was made by a man named Tom Ponting. He shaped up a herd in Texas, trailed it to Illinois, fattened it on grass throughout the winter, and then pushed all the way to New York City.

From 1852 to 1854 Texas cattle were also trailed to Arkansas, Kansas, Nebraska, Missouri, and Iowa. After 1857 several long drives were made to Memphis, Tennessee. But St. Louis remained a prime market. A fat steer could bring as high as thirty dollars in gold there.

The future looked very bright. There was an inexhaustible supply of Texas cattle. No amount of trailing thousands to market seemed to make a dent in their number. There was ready access to markets along the Texas Road. Eastern cattle could not begin to supply the fast-growing cities there. Railroads, ever pushing westward, speeded the delivery of cattle from west to east.

But then the bright bubble burst. The movement of cattle from Texas was hamstrung by a grim "fever war" and then cut off completely at the outbreak of the Civil War.

After the smoke of battle cleared, Texas cattle had to find a new trail north.

Nowadays, few remember the beginnings of the Texas Road, and its role in the history of American cattle trails. But those who ride the Missouri, Kansas and Texas Railroad, or drive over US Highway 69 from northeastern Oklahoma to Texas can look out across the ancient trace, though the ruts worn by those cattle of long ago have been covered with crops, steel rails, and concrete highways.

5

The Fever War

The fever war did not start suddenly. Like other wars, it broke out after long grumbling and harsh words between men.

From 1830 on, when Texas cattle were trailed north, wherever they trod beyond the Red River, domesticated shorthorn cattle sickened and died after their passing. The farmers along the Texas Road, both Indian and white and particularly those in Arkansas and Missouri, claimed the Texas cattle were diseased. Yet any one could see they were robust and healthy! But there was no doubting the grim fact that wherever Texas cattle appeared—to be fattened on good grass in Illinois and Ohio, or even as far off as New York— within a month after their arrival, milk cows and good beef stock died. In some places there were widespread epidemics of this so-called "Texas fever," and several thousand cattle died. But the fatalities were always northern cattle.

One thing became obvious. Whatever dread scourge the Longhorns carried, they themselves were immune to it.

There were all sorts of explanations for the sickness. Some claimed it was spread by the Longhorns' urine and dung. Others said their saliva contaminated the grass. Still others were positive that the dead ticks, falling from the Longhorn's heavily-infested hides, dropped to the grass and when eaten by domesticated cattle, sickened them. But as time passed, more and more people became convinced that the trouble came from the live ticks transferred from southern to northern cattle. The end result was always the same—disaster. It was more than disheartening. To many it was catastrophic. Quite naturally it bred increasing dislike for the Texas breed.

The symptoms were always the same. About four weeks after being exposed to Longhorns, the northern cattle would begin to refuse to eat. They would arch their backs; they burned with fever; their blood turned to water; their ribs stuck out. Yes, they did seem to be swarming with the little red-brown ticks. Finally, the cattle dropped to their knees, and died. Men were afraid to eat the diseased meat. All they could save were the hides. And then they had the sad and backbreaking work of burying the bloated animals.

"Any fool can see our cattle aren't to blame," protested the Texans. "See, they're still as fat and healthy as ever, and they've been feeding right alongside these dead ones."

Some of the Texans claimed their cattle were being blamed for the trouble simply because northerners didn't like southern cattle dominating so much of the cattle market, and enriching Texans.

Then in June 1853, when some Texas cattle were being driven peaceably across Vernon County, in western Missouri, the cowboys were astounded to find the trail blocked by a grim company of riders armed with pitchforks and guns.

"What's this all about?" they demanded.

"Turn those cattle back," the Missourians demanded.

An argument developed. The Missourians raised their weapons. The Texans, outnumbered, grumblingly turned back down the trail several miles, located a different passage, and finally after much

trouble got back on the main trail. But they were forced aside again and again on their way to market.

Other drovers were not so lucky. They were not only turned back, but some were tied up and horsewhipped for bringing Longhorns into the region. Some had their stock gunned down. In several counties the farmers formed protective associations. They deputized officers to arrest and fine any Texans who appeared on the scene.

But Texans still persisted in pushing their herds north. So on December 15, 1855, Missouri passed a quarantine law which barred Texas cattle from that state, and promised stockmen they would be fined twenty-five dollars for every animal they brought up the trail.

But enforcement of the law was left to local officers, who accepted bribes to let the Longhorns pass, and so the fever continued. The disease abated for some seasons, then came on strong again. In June 1859, armed, angry farmers turned back three herds numbering two thousand Longhorns. The Clinton, Missouri *Journal* editorialized: "No one can for a moment blame the citizens of Missouri for adopting summary measures to protect their stock from the fearful ravages of Spanish fever."

The Texans sought to avoid Missouri altogether, and trailed their herds straight north up through extreme eastern Kansas. When thousands of Kansas cattle died, their owners barred the trail. The Kansas Legislature passed a law barring all Texas, Arkansas, and

Indian cattle from passing through four eastern counties between June 1 and November 1. Rifle companies were formed to make the law work.

The outbreak of the Civil War in 1861 stopped all northbound movement of cattle. The Texas stock was needed to supply Confederate troops. By the thousands, cattle were moved across Texas to the Mississippi river, and were shipped to southern ports and throughout the south. And wherever they went, they spread the fever. But so great was the demand for meat and leather, that little protest was heard about the fever.

When trailing Longhorns north resumed after the war was over, it was the same old story. Texas cattle trailed to Illinois brought on an epidemic that cost the farmers hundreds of thousands of dollars. Those sent to new markets at Abilene, Kansas over the new trails still brought sickness and death in their wake.

Then the Texans got a taste of the misery they had caused. In an effort to improve and upgrade the quality of their rangy beasts, they began importing hundreds and hundreds of fine, well-bred shorthorns from the north. As soon as these newcomers hit the Texas ranches, they sickened and died. Veterinarians were brought in to study the diseased cattle, and find out how to eradicate the fever, but none of these men discovered what caused the trouble. The scourge went on and on, even until the 1890's, with no one coming close to solving the problem.

Then Theobald Smith arrived on the scene.

He was a young man, a doctor, well trained for those times, and avid to do research. He accepted a position with a new, weak, struggling Bureau of Animal Industry in Washington, D.C. At that time, there were only four men on the staff: the director, an assistant named Kilborne, Smith, and a former slave who washed bottles and tended the laboratory animals.

"Find out what is causing Texas fever," the director ordered Smith. It was a mammoth task that could take years. Smith was delighted. He set up a laboratory in an attic room of a government building. He dissected diseased cattle livers and spleens, but learned little. "Find the germ!" the director pressed. Summer was coming on, and the attic was like an oven. It was also overrun with cockroaches.

Smith studied all that had been written about the fever. Being a sensible man, he also listened to what cattlemen said. They vowed that the ticks caused the disease.

To prove this, Smith would have to move his laboratory outside. And this is exactly what he did. He chose an area outside of Washington, and fenced off six fields. He had seven healthy southern cows delivered. On June 7, 1889, into Field #1 he placed four of these cows. They were heavily infested with ticks. Some of the ticks were so small they could only be seen under a magnifying glass. Others were swollen with blood sucked from the cows, and measured a half-inch in length. In with these four tick-ridden cows, Smith put six healthy northern cattle.

Next, Smith and his assistant picked off with their hands every tick they could find on the three remaining southern cows. It wasn't easy. The cows twitched and turned. They switched their tails in Smith's face. They kicked up dust, which added to the discomfort the scientists were suffering in one-hundred-degree-plus summer heat. But Smith and Kilborne persisted. They filled bottles with the tiny or blood-gorged parasites. When the three cows were clean, they placed them in Field #2, along with four healthy northern cattle. "Now maybe we can find out whether the ticks really are to blame," Smith said.

All the cows in the experiment would be eating the same grass, drinking the same water, rubbing sides, sniffing each other.

While waiting to find out which cows would come down with the fever, Smith and another government scientist, an expert named Cooper Curtice, studied the ticks. They found how the six-legged back tick climbs up on a cow, fastens itself to the hide, sucks blood, sheds its skin, acquires two more legs, and sheds again. They watched the eight-legged females mate on the cow's back with a small male tick, then engorge themselves with blood, drop off the cow to the ground, and lay some two thousand eggs. After this the females shriveled and died, the entire cycle consuming only some twenty days. After the eggs hatched, the small ticks crawled around until they found a cow, and attached themselves to it, repeating the cycle.

Every day Smith found time to return to his fields. He saw the ticks get on to the healthy northern cows in Field #1. He picked off the few ticks that popped up on the healthy southern cows in Field #2. This was a hot, dusty, sweaty, and dull job, but he followed it through with great zeal. Soon the healthy northern cows in Field #1 sickened. One by one they died. Their tick-laden bodies dropped to the ground.

But the northern cows in Field #2 acquired no ticks, and remained very healthy! August passed. September waned. They stayed well. To be sure of his findings, Smith led two of them into tick-infested Field #1. In a few weeks, they were dead.

Meantime Smith had spent long hours in the suffocating attic, bent over his microscope. He saw that the unknown Texas fever microbe attacked the blood corpuscles of the cows, turning them to water.

From North Carolina, where there were many ticks, he received large cans of grass which was crawling with the parasites. He distributed this grass in Field #3, where there had been neither ticks nor cows, southern or northern. Then he put four northern cows in this field. In a few weeks they humped their backs and burned with fever. Two died, but two recovered after a severe bout.

It must be the tick!

But Smith wanted still more proof. He repeated his experiments during the summer of 1890, and solved the mystery of how the ticks get from one southern cow to a northern cow. He had thousands of ticks gathered, and fed them in hay to healthy northern cows. Nothing happened. He ground up ticks into soup and drenched another cow with the foul mess. Nothing happened. He kept asking himself, "Why does it take thirty days or more for the fever to appear?"

Stockmen told him they could mix newly-arrived southern cows with northern cows, and if they were separated within twenty days, the disease did not appear. He even hatched clean baby ticks in the laboratory, and placed them on a fat heifer. She died. He tried other tricks, not all successful. But finally he came on a great discovery: it was not the old female tick, but the baby tick, five to ten days old, who wreaked the havoc. Now he knew why it took so long for the fever to break out after the animal came in contact with ticks: the mother ticks first had to drop off the southern cattle, lay their eggs, and die; the newly-hatched ticks had to find a cow's leg to crawl up, fasten themselves to the hide, and begin sucking blood before the damage set in.

Then Smith asked himself another question: did this happen only in the summer, as stockmen claimed, or could it happen in winter? After Christmas he placed laboratory-raised ticks on a heifer kept in a warm stable. She died.

For two more summers Smith and Kilborne conducted experiments. They found northern calves contracted only mild cases of the fever, and after that were immune to it. It was already obvious that decades of calves produced by immune cows had made the southern cattle immune to tick fever.

But the ticks were everywhere. What could the ranchers do? More experiments followed. Finally it was discovered that dipping cattle regularly in a bath of creosote and other ingredients killed the ticks. Texas cattlemen, as well as northern operators, were willing to do this to be rid of the costly scourge. Although by this time trailing cattle from the south to the north had been discontinued, due to the coming of the railroads throughout the nation, cattlemen no longer needed to fear southern cattle. Tick fever became a thing of the past.

6

Cattle and the Civil War

While the fever war set cattleman against cattleman along the Texas Road, another more terrible war between the north and the south pinched off all trailing of cattle between the two sections of the country.

Soon after the War Between the States was declared, President Abraham Lincoln proclaimed a blockade of the coasts of the seceding states. This did not affect the southeastern market for Texas beef because Texas declared herself wholeheartedly for the Confederate cause. On August 16, 1861, the President prohibited further trade between the north and the south, cutting off the Kansas and Missouri market for the Texas Longhorns.

Next the Secretary of War closed a number of garrisons situated near the Texas Road, and particularly those in Texas. As the officers and troops moved north for re-assignment at Fort Leavenworth, in Kansas, there were wholesale desertions by those who supported the southern cause. This recall was a foolish move on the part of the Union Army because it left the Indian Nations open to Confederate control. It endangered the Creeks, and many Cherokees who sympathized with the north, leaving them vulnerable to raids by slave-holding Choctaws and Chickasaws who swung to the opposing side. While the north made no effort to enlist the help of the Indian nations, the south did, promising that after the war was won, the Indian nations would be formed into a separate state, with rights equal to those of whites, including the right to vote.

Cattlemen suffered because regardless of which cause they supported, their herds were harassed or seized by those on the other side. The movement of cattle on the Texas Road ground to a halt, save for that of Confederate sympathizers supplying southern troops. So many Texans marched off to war that the cattle industry was neglected. The women and children tried hard, but they could not cope with the branding and roundups.

Before long the Confederate Congress realized something had to be done, as much as the south now was dependent on Texas beef and hides. So it permitted a limited number of stockmen to be exempt from the draft, supposedly one man for every five hundred head of cattle. It also set a price of twenty-five dollars a head for every beef trailed east through Louisiana and southern Arkansas and across the Mississippi River. But when the New Orleans market was cut off by the Union Army in the spring of 1862, and federal gunboats prowled the river, moving Texas beef across the Mississippi became an exceedingly chancy business.

Unaware that New Orleans was in Union hands, and eager to serve the Confederate Army which he was too young to join, a slim Texas lad named W. D. H. Saunders determined to move a herd east from his home near Goliad. With two young friends, Jim Borroum and Monroe Choate, and some others, he started out with eight hundred Longhorn steers. All crossed the Guadalupe River safely near Clinton, but in Lavaca county the cattle stampeded. It took days to round them up. Moving on, they crossed the Colorado

River at Columbus, the Brazos near Richmond, the Trinity near Liberty, the Natches at Beaumont, and the Sabine near Orange. In Louisiana they swung around Opelousas, a good-sized cattle market. Here they were joined by two more trail drivers with three hundred steers. The combined herd continued east, until stopped by gray uniformed cavalry.

"Where are y'all bound for?" the officer demanded.

"New Orleans," Saunders answered promptly.

The officer snapped, "You're under arrest!"

"Arrest? What for?"

"For aiding and abetting the Yankees by transporting beef to them!"

Saunders and his friends were astounded. This was the first they knew about New Orleans being in enemy hands. Try as they did, they could not convince the officer of their good intentions. The whole kit and caboodle was moved, under guard, to Alexandria, Louisiana, to stand courtmartial trial. Fortunately the presiding officer had better sense, and released the boys, with a warning to stay north of New Orleans.

Where could he take the cattle now, Saunders wondered. Mobile, Alabama was a good place, but too far away. Yet directly across the Mississippi, Confederate troops were desperately in need of beef. The boys talked it over. The river was a mile wide at this point, and some forty feet deep. There was no ferry. A Yankee gunboat might run them down.

Nevertheless Saunders did not hesitate, though his young face was grim. "Lead 'em out!" he ordered.

His friends drove the steers toward the brown, roiling river. Saunders splashed in. His horse went under, and both came up, blowing. The other cowboys yelled and swung their ropes, and drove the cattle into the water. The leaders balked at first, but were crowded off the bank. The rest plunged in, churning the muddy water to a creamy foam. Some of the riders rode on the flanks, to help keep the herd together; others followed to the rear. Chances were that all would be lost in the crossing. No older man with a hoot

of sense would have tried it. But the young lads did, yowling and whistling and swinging their ropes to keep the cattle swimming.

When the lead steers felt the full force of the strong current, they tried to turn back. Saunders knew this would be fatal. The herd would swim in circles until each animal tired, and drowned. Quickly Saunders kneed his horse so it came upstream from the lead steer. When the animal saw him, the cowboy yelled and swung his quirt and pointed for the far shore. Although the steer's eyes were rolling with fright, it kept on swimming and followed Saunders. The mile seemed endless. Many times Saunders looked back, and grinned when he saw the countless horns bobbing in the water. The last

hundred yards were the hardest. Horses and cattle were wall-eyed, panting, exhausted, but they did not give up. Soon the first ones were stumbling wearily onto the bank. There they stood, trembling, heads down, unable to move a foot farther.

"We made it!" Saunders whooped as all but one hundred of the cattle and all the men came out of the river.

After a rest, with time out to wring out their clothing and make coffee from the beans one cowboy had carried in his hat, the drive got underway again, moving across Louisiana toward the Mississippi state line. Here they were accosted by more troops, and this time Saunders and his friends were thrown into the guard house, for aiding the enemy! It took several days and a great deal of palavering to convince the military authorities of their loyalty to the south. But finally Saunders and company were released, and went on to the market at Woodville, and sold their stock. After returning home, Saunders helped his mother run the family spread. As soon as he was old enough, he enlisted in the Confederate Army. The story of his great feat was told all over Texas, then and for years afterwards.

Another hero was Colonel D. H. Snyder who worked tirelessly throughout the war, moving cattle from Texas almost to the battle-fields. Sometimes his herds were ferried across rivers on barges, but in time Snyder trained two steers as leaders. When they came to a river, and there were numerous rivers to cross on the way, the two lead steers plunged right in and swam toward the opposite bank. Normally, when a herd reaches its destination, every animal is sold. But Snyder retained his two intelligent lead steers, trailed them home, and used them time and time again in his efforts to get meat to the soldiers. After the fall of Vicksburg in July 1863, the Mississippi was brought under federal control. No more Texas cattle reached the troops, and the Confederate soldiers slowly starved.

Since there was little branding of calves during the war, and marketing came to a standstill, the Longhorns multiplied almost beyond belief. With their owners gone to war, many semi-domesticated herds took to roaming and reverted to the wild state. Even a widespread drouth that prostrated Texas in 1863 and 1864 seemed to have little effect on their number. By 1865, supposedly six million cattle were roaming freely in Texas. This was ironic because up north so many cattle had been taken to feed the Union Army that in many areas, cattle were almost non-existent. Even milk cows were scarce. What a situation! Too many cattle in Texas, too few up north, and hostilities preventing the obvious solution to the problem.

Soldiers throughout the south returned home to a ravaged land, to abandoned plantations, fields overgrown with weeds, and broken fences. Seed was not available, nor breeding stock to start new herds. The Negroes, freed from bondage, were unwilling to work in the cotton fields. The south was bankrupt.

According to statistics gathered at the time, it was determined that eighty cattle were needed for each one hundred people, and this ratio maintained constantly if people were to be adequately supplied. Therefore the New England states needed some 785,000 cattle, the Middle states one and a half million, and the south, excluding Texas, a like number. New York, Pennsylvania, New Jersey, Delaware, Maryland, and Virginia were crying for cattle. Then to complicate matters, when Middle West farmers returned from the war, they did not resume raising livestock. A new invention, the McCormick wheat reaper, and other labor-saving agricultural machinery, made them change over from a beef crop to a wheat and corn crop. Prices for scarce beef rose so high that few could afford to buy.

When the Texas cattlemen learned this, they realized that the only, and the quickest, way back to economic recovery for themselves and their state was to get busy with rope and branding iron, and move the mature beeves out on the north-bound trail. Although they hated the thought of doing business with the north after their humiliating defeat, there was no other solution. Texas was bulging with cattle. The north was strapped for them.

Once more fires smoked, ropes sung, and whips cracked. Working in heat, dust, and mud, pestered by mosquitos and rattlesnakes, the cowmen began rounding up herds. One youngster named Lee Moore described a cow hunt in 1865:

"Every man on this cow hunt was a cattle owner just home from the war who went out to see what he had left to brand. I was the only boy on this cow hunt and was looking for cattle that belonged to my father before the war. We had no wagon. Every man carried his grub in a wallet on behind his saddle and his bed under his saddle. I was put on herd and carried a lot of extra wallets behind my saddle and a string of tin cups on a hobble around my pony's neck. A wallet is a sack with both ends sewed up, with the mouth in the middle. Whenever the boss herder couldn't hear those cups jingling, he would come around and wake me up.

"We would corral those cattle every night at some one of the owners' homes and stand guard around the corral. I didn't stand guard but carried brush and cornstalks and anything I could get to make a light for those who were on guard . . . Every few days they would divide and brand and each man take his cattle home. The cow hunt lasted all summer."

In the spring of 1866 the herds were ready for the long walk north. One newspaper complained, "The boys, as soon as they can climb on a pony, are off to the prairie to drive stock. As they advance toward manhood, their highest ambition is to conquer a pitching mustang or throw a wild beef by the tail."

The expected road dangers were not the only ones to be faced. Kansas still had her dander up about Texas fever, and would permit no herds to pass through the eastern part of the state. So a good many herds were driven across the Red River, and on past Boggy Depot on the old Texas Road. But there they swung west of the Kansas settlements before turning north, and thus avoided a showdown with vigilance committees.

One cattleman has left a diary of the trouble encountered on the 1866 drive. He was George C. Duffield, an Iowa farmer who had gone to Texas and bought a herd. On April 29, he left the Austin area with several hundred head. The beeves stampeded three times in the next eight days, causing a great deal of trouble in rounding them up. Then heavy rain slowed the pace. Some of the camp equipment was lost crossing the swollen Brazos, and a rider drowned in the Red River. Of the Boggy Depot region, he wrote, "We hauled cattle out of the mud with oxen all day." Indians stole some near Fort Gibson, and more were lost in the Arkansas. In southeastern Kansas, Duffield headed west, then north, slogged through northeastern Nebraska and pushed eastward into Iowa. By October 31, he came into Ottumwa, Iowa with the remnants. He shipped one hundred cattle by rail to Burlington, to fatten on the farm, and put the remainder through to the packing house at Chicago.

At least a quarter of a million cattle crossed the Red River that year, heading north. The drovers paid toll in beeves, since they lacked cash, to the Indians whose territory they crossed. They tried to avoid the fever patrols, and if stopped, put up with considerable verbal abuse because they knew they had to get their herds to market.

Nineteen-year-old Jim Daugherty of Denton County, Texas was

one of the unlucky ones. To avoid paying toll to the Indians, he turned his herd east into Arkansas and followed the line north to Missouri. Part way he came upon several herds being held up by renegades who had killed one drover, and stolen many cattle. Leaving his stock with his five-man crew, he rode on alone to Fort Scott, where he sold his cattle. Then he returned to move them up the last lap.

Suddenly Daugherty found his party surrounded by Jayhawkers, coonskin-capped outlaws who preyed on farmers and drovers alike. One of Jim's riders drew his pistol, but was shot out of his saddle. The troublemakers flapped blankets, and stampeded the cattle. When Daugherty tried to prevent this, he was roped and dragged to the nearest tree. The Jayhawkers argued whether or not to hang him, and finally decided to strip his back bare and whip him with hickory switches. After that, they rode away.

Although suffering intensely, Daugherty managed to work himself free; he found his horse, and rode back to see if he had any friends or cattle left. Surprisingly enough, he did. His men had managed to round up all but about one hunded and fifty head. After taking time to bury the murdered rider, and by moving at night, Jim got his herd through to Fort Scott without further incident.

The cattle kept coming, in spite of tolls, renegades, fever patrols, and a newly-established quarantine against Texas cattle in western and northern Kansas counties. Some turned west at Baxter Springs, Kansas, and went north into Nebraska, or across Missouri into Iowa. Others tried going up the Missouri line, and cutting across to Sedalia. This portion of the trail from the Red River to Sedalia was called the Sedalia Trail. Since the Kansas quarantine was in effect only from May until November 1, some cattlemen held their stock on the pastures of friendly Cherokees in Oklahoma, and did not lead them north until the vigilantes withdrew from the trail. But blizzards caught them enroute, and many cattle died.

In 1867 five more states passed laws restricting the trailing of Texas and Indian cattle across their borders: Missouri, Nebraska, Colorado, Illinois, and Kentucky. As badly as they needed cattle, the farmers of these states were determined to keep out the fever-bearing Longhorns.

But the law of one state, Kansas, had a loophole in it, a geographical loophole: the southwestern part of the state was left open to drovers. The cowmen even were allowed to take their cattle from this free region, on north to shipping points on the Kansas Pacific railroad. They had to keep their herds off the public highways; they had to pay a bond as guarantee of payment for damage to property, or to compensate for any local stock dying later of the fever; they had to stay five miles out from any settlement.

On learning of this loophole, the much-troubled Texas cattlemen took hope. Now they had a way to reach the northern market. Charlie Goodnight opened one trail to market, and Jesse Chisholm an even better one.

7

Goodnight-Loving Trail
Texas to New Mexico and Colorado

Charlie Goodnight sat his horse on a golden stretch of mesquite grass in the Palo Pinto country, along the Brazos in north central Texas. His mouth was grim, his legs taut against saddle leather. At sun-up that morning, he and his hands had looked out over three thousand cattle. They were a mixed lot gathered the hard way off the prairie, or at a watering place, or out of the brush, and branded with his CV brand. Now there were only a thousand left. The Comanches had roared down on his outfit, letting out their arrows and wild whoops and flapping blankets. They had killed his best point man, thrown the herd into an uproar, and because of their superior numbers, had gotten away with two thousand head. He and his men were exhausted from trying to repel the attack and turn the remnant back to the home grazing ground. Worse, this wasn't the first time he'd lost a herd to the Comanches.

An ordinary man would have given up. But not Charlie Goodnight, who had ridden bareback from Illinois to Texas when he was nine, and had bowed legs to show for it; not the young man who had fought in a war and been a Texas Ranger, and now was trying, against terrible odds of postwar depression, little money, and Indian raids, to make his stake in the cattle business. A Charlie Goodnight didn't give up as long as he could sit a horse. He swallowed his disappointment, and got to work building his herd again.

By the spring of 1866 Goodnight was ready to hit the trial again. He had listened to a lot of talk from those who were going to run the gauntlet of tolls through the Indian nations, of raids by Jayhawkers, of blockades by angry, armed Kansas farmers. He'd heard others talk about running their cattle south, across the Rio Grande and deep into Mexico to a weak market.

The only bright story was the one he had heard about George Reynolds. Young Reynolds had rounded up a herd, given his IOU for eight dollars a head to the ranchers who let him have the critters on credit, and then squeaked them through to New Mexico, where they were sold to the government for sixty dollars a head. Of course, Reynolds had started way south in the Big Bend country, had come up the good side of the Pecos, and had faced no Indians all the way to Fort Sumner. The cattle buyers gathered there to purchase beef for the Indian reservations and the military posts strung through the wilderness. The government had to provide beef for the Indians to keep them off the warpath. Since cattle were scarce, the price for trail-toughened steers was high.

Sixty dollars a head. Goodnight thought hard on it. If a man could bring a thousand head or more into Fort Sumner, he'd make himself a mighty nice piece of money. A flinty smile crinkled his cheeks. But not for long. When he mentioned to his closest friends, all cattlemen, that he had an idea about driving a herd to New Mexico, they said, "Impossible." Not because of the Comanches. The country he would have to cross between the Palo Pinto and New Mexico was so desolate that the Indians avoided it! Nevertheless he proposed to take cattle over it. There was a cruel ninety-six-mile waterless stretch that no herd could cross, and survive. Or so his friends said.

But Goodnight could not be convinced. He knew Longhorns. He was sure he knew how he could get them across. He tried to get others to join him on the desperate task. None would hear of it. Then Goodnight talked with fifty-year-old Oliver Loving, the most respected and experienced trail driver in all Texas. Loving had blazed the trail from the Red River to Sedalia, Missouri. He had pushed another herd all the way to Colorado. During the war he had moved plenty of beef to the Confederate Army, and that was saying a lot. Now he was broke. The war had done that to him. But he had lots of company in his poverty. Goodnight for one.

The two got busy. They rounded up two thousand cattle, a mixed herd of cows, steers, and calves. They traded for horses, and hired eighteen hands, every one a war veteran. Most of them still were wearing parts of their uniforms. Then Goodnight, without realizing it, made a great innovation. Instead of packing the grub and gear on horses or in a wagon, he designed the first chuckwagon ever to be used. It was a large wagon of yellow wood equipped with water barrels, a kitchen cabinet with drawers for flour, coffee, sugar, spices, tinware, pots, and room left over for bedrolls, ropes, and the thousand and one things needed on a long hard drive. He yoked ten pair of oxen to it, and put the wagon in the charge of a crusty character who chewed tobacco and made the lightest sourdough biscuits in Texas.

They started out, Goodnight way in front, scouting the trail, waving his hat to signal the pointers, the men riding at the head of the herd. Loving was everywhere, constantly circling the herd, keeping a good pace. But even though the Texas prairie made for easy going at first, there was trouble. The calves could not keep up. Goodnight put them in the chuckwagon, where they blatted loudly, which made the mothers butt the wagon. Within a couple of weeks more calves were born, too many for the over-burdened wagon. Goodnight and Loving had to make a tough decision. They had to kill the calves. Goodnight hated having to do it. "I'll never take a mixed herd over this route again," he vowed.

The herd moved from the upper Brazos to the Middle Concho. There the stock rested, and drank. All canteens and water barrels were filled. When the sun was in the west, and the most intense heat of the day gone, Goodnight called, "Line 'em out!" The waterless stretch lay ahead.

As the herd toiled across the dry plains, bitter alkali dust rose about them, all but blinding and suffocating both men and animals. They trailed late, made a dry camp, and were on the way again at the first streak of light in the east. The second day the herd was restless from thirst. That night the animals milled and bawled, and refused to rest. Goodnight seemed to suffer with them. The men were saddle sore and very tired. Loving had worked the drag all day in a desperate effort to keep the cattle from turning back. His fatigue was bone deep, his eyes bloodshot.

When daylight came, the herd was still milling. They had walked enough miles to have reached water, and all in a futile circle. "Move 'em out," Loving and Goodnight told their men.

The leaders tried to forge ahead. Goodnight rode back and forth, from point to flank. By midday the men were parched, their lips cracked, their kerchiefs caked with dust, and their clothes sweat soaked. The water barrels were dry. The canteens were drained. The cattle were in terrible condition. They were dehydrated. Their ribs stuck out, as did their swollen tongues. They were getting spookier with every mile. Their bawling grated on the men's fraz-

zled nerves. The cowboys, hoarse from calling, tore buttons off their clothing and sucked them, to make saliva flow in their mouths.

On the third day the cattle started dropping by the trail. The men could hardly stay in their saddles. And still Goodnight waved them on. Having ridden ahead, only Goodnight knew of a new danger up the trail. There were pools of water off to the side, deadly water, so full of alkali that a few swallows would kill a man or an animal. Now he had the extra burden of turning the herd farther west. He managed it, and the outfit trudged on. Then even the cowboys dropped to the ground. Although his own horse was stumbling, Goodnight called a halt.

"Get some sleep if you can," he told the weakest men. He gathered up all the canteens. "I'm going for water."

No one protested. None had voice left, or strength to accompany him. He rode off across the burning plain. It was ten miles to the river, and the sight made his heart sink. Water, yes, but it ran below twenty-foot banks! Once his cattle got a whiff of the water, they'd roll their eyes and tails, and take out like wild things. They'd run pell mell off the bank and pile up in the water . . . unless the men could string them out along the bank.

Quickly Goodnight filled the canteens, and with horse and man revived somewhat from drinking, he returned to camp. The men swigged the water gratefully. Goodnight told them what they had to do. They nodded numbly, wiped their faces on their kerchiefs. After a talk, Goodnight and Loving decided to let the stronger cattle forge ahead. Loving would stay with the drags. Goodnight, as usual, would take the lead. He watched the lead animals closely. He saw the first moment when they sniffed the water, saw them bawl, stretch their necks, and begin to line out in a faltering, crazed run. The point riders tried to hold them back. The earth thundered under their hooves. They poured down on the river in a gray cloud. The leaders went over the bank into the water. With others falling on top of them, they kept swimming. Even in the water, the point riders kept waving their arms and yelling, "Hi-yah, hi-yah!" to get them to spread out. Slowly, they foundered in the shallows, strung out, stood heaving and blowing, their tongues dripping water. Several hours passed before the herd had drunk its fill, and was grazing on river-bottom grass along the far shore.

But soon the air was rent with noise. The weaker cattle approached, with Loving cracking a whip at the rear. They ran over each other, and plunged into the water. Some drowned. Others floundered fatally into quicksand. It was impossible to rescue them. Although the cowboys worked hard for two days, over one hundred cattle died at or in the Pecos River. Goodnight tallied the survivors. So far they had lost 500 head, counting the calves killed and the ones rotting back on the trail.

When the herd was rested, the journey across more dry, desolate country resumed. But the worst was behind them. They finished the seven-hundred-mile trek in fair shape.

The residents of Fort Sumner whooped with joy at the sight of the cattle. There were 8,500 hungry Indians lolling about the fort, in addition to the military and civilian staff. So the two partners had no difficulty disposing of one thousand steers for $12,000 in gold coins and certificates.

"Twelve thousand dollars!" Goodnight exclaimed, his voice choked with wonder. He had left Texas a poor man. Now he had a fine stake, and he and Loving still had five hundred of the weaker cows and steers left.

At Fort Sumner, the two learned that a strong market for beef had developed up in Colorado, thanks to a gold strike in the Denver area. After a rest, Loving suggested, "Why don't we take the rest of the herd up there?"

"Good idea," his partner agreed. "But we both don't need to go. I'll go back to Texas, and bring out another herd to the fort."

Loving eyed him. "You'd go through all that misery again?"

Goodnight nodded. He would. What's more, he would do a better job now that he had blazed the trail. He would select only sturdy, mature steers who could travel faster and endure more than a mixed herd. "I'll be back here in the fall," he promised.

"What about robbers?" Loving said worriedly. The news of the sale was common knowledge around the fort. There were several disreputable men hanging about.

The two made plans in secret. They selected three top hands to accompany Goodnight. They stuffed their saddle bags with coffee, beans, and tinned biscuits. The gold was packed on a sturdy mule. Long after dark, when the fort was quiet, Goodnight and his men made a fast, forced ride, and put as many miles as possible between them and the fort. At daylight they holed up in the brush. They made no fire, and were not discovered by any Indians. They rode two more nights, and hid out during the daylight hours. But one night a terrible electrical storm raked the country. Lightning bolts hammered the earth on all sides. The thunder rumbled like cannon fire. One bolt of lightning hit too close to the pack mule. It reared. Goodnight made a wild leap, and caught its neck rope. The mule plunged, kicked, and bolted away from the campsite. Goodnight held on grimly. By the time the mule quieted, he was badly skinned and bruised, but he had saved the gold. The remainder of the journey was made without trouble.

Meanwhile Loving had pushed the herd northward from Fort Sumner over eight-thousand-foot high, boulder-strewn Raton Pass. He had no trouble, however, because for some years there had been an improved trail of sorts over the pass as far as the Arkansas River. This was a portion of the much-traveled Santa Fe Trail. Since the Cheyennes beyond were friendly to whites, the cowman had no difficulty taking his herd the rest of the way into Denver. As expected, he sold them for a good price.

Back in Texas, cattlemen were astonished to hear Goodnight tell how he had trailed cattle over a southern route to New Mexico. They were torn between fear of the waterless stretch, and the fat profits that could be realized now that the Goodnight-Loving Trail, as it was called, was marked, and the mileages known.

For a second time Goodnight threw a herd on the trail. The steers were harder to handle, having no cows along to help quiet them, but the sturdy beasts did travel faster. But then, as always, trouble appeared. A long, long line of buffalo migrating southward hove into view. They got wind of the steers, and began to snort. Goodnight and his men tried to turn back their herd, so as to let the buffalo pass. It was too late. The buffalo stampeded right through Goodnight's cattle. The steers rolled their tails, and took off east and west, while the buffalo raced through them. For over an hour, there was bedlam. Finally the last of the buffalos passed, and Goodnight's crew began the wearying task of rounding up their badly-scattered cattle. It was an exhausting, time-consuming task, hard on horses and men. When all was in order again, and the steers counted, Goodnight was relieved to learn that not one steer had been lost.

When they approached the dry stretch, Goodnight gave the steers all the grass and water they could hold. He started at sundown, and made a hard drive all night. In the cool of the morning, he stopped long enough for the animals to graze, and for his men to eat and get a little rest. Then he pushed on, at a slower pace because of the heat, but steadily. The third afternoon they came to a stop two miles from Fort Sumner. Loving was there to greet them.

The two men cleared a dugout in the river bank and furnished it with crude home-made furniture. They spent the winter comfortably, selling the herd piecemeal to the buyers. In the very early spring the two slipped out one dark night with their accumulated gold. They returned safely to Texas, with money enough to buy prime steers, and shape up another herd of two thousand.

They started out again with high hopes. For the first few days of the forty-day trek, all went well. After that, it was trouble, trouble, trouble. A large band of Comanches stampeded the herd on Clear Fork, not once, but twice. One cowboy got an arrow behind his ear. But he was still alive. Goodnight ordered, "Hold him down." He dug the cruel barb from the cowboy's head. Then he poulticed the wound with mud. After a few hours' rest, during which time the crew rounded up the stampeded cattle, the cowboy was ready to ride again.

Farther on, the Comanches struck twice more. Many days were spent chasing the cattle out of the brush. The steers, now used to running, were owly-eyed and very hard to handle.

Loving was worried, knowing other cattle were on the trail ahead of them. Goodnight and Loving no longer would have the market all to themselves, as they had the previous years. "We're going to be too late for the bidding at Fort Sumner," Loving said, referring to a certain date when government contractors bought beef. "I'd better go ahead on my own, so we'll have some one at the sale."

Goodnight refused. He would not hear of Loving's traveling alone through the Indian-infested country. But finally, much against his better judgment, Goodnight assented. "You're not going alone. You take One-Arm Wilson with you." One-Arm was a hard-bitten, gritty cowboy who could ride and shoot well, even though crippled. "Promise me you'll travel at night, and hole up in the brush during the day. It's the only way you'll get through without losing your hair."

Loving agreed. Shortly after he and the cowboy set out on their horses, with a little dried meat and biscuit in their saddlebags. For forty-eight hours they were careful. But because they hadn't come across any fresh Indian sign, the two decided to chance riding in the daytime. They could make much better time. It looked like they might make it. But as they approached the Pecos, a small band of Comanches jumped them. Loving and Wilson flung shots at their pursuers, and raced for the thickets. They managed to hide, but not before Loving had gotten one bullet through his wrist, and another through his side. He was in bad shape.

"You go on," he insisted, wincing with pain. He had lost a lot of blood. "I can't ride. Maybe you can get back to Goodnight, and bring help."

At first Wilson was reluctant to leave. At last he saw there was no choice. Loving was too badly injured to ride. Where one man might slip past the Comanches, two could not. He made Loving as comfortable as possible, reloaded his rifle and waist gun, and said good-bye. Miraculously, he reached Goodnight.

Goodnight pushed the herd as hard as he dared, but it was several days before they reached the Pecos. When Wilson led him to where he had left Loving, the wounded man was not to be found.

Strong man though he was, Goodnight blanched with fear. Had

the Indians caught his friend alive? If so, they would wreak unspeakable torture on the helpless white man. But the more Goodnight thought about it, the more he thought this might not have happened. Loving would never have allowed himself to be taken alive. Deeply worried, Goodnight moved to the fort.

"Has any one seen Loving?" was the first question he asked.

The answer was yes. Loving had escaped the Indians and met some Mexicans who took him to the fort. He lay seriously ill in the barrack's room. Goodnight hastened to his side. One look at Loving's arm told him the worst. The wound had not been properly tended. Gangrene had set in. In spite of an emergency amputation, the good man died.

Then Goodnight had more trouble. The cattle had arrived too late for the sale. So Goodnight pushed the herd on up a north-flowing creek, pointing for Colorado. However, on the way he came onto a twenty-mile canyon, not too steep, with a fine grassy bottom and creek, the Apishapa. It was a natural corral. Goodnight tarried there, and rode its length. Blast the Indians, anyway, he thought. They had killed his best friend. They had plundered his herd time and time again. They promised more trouble if he stayed on in the Palo Duro country, in Texas. Why butt his head against such heavy odds? Why risk death daily, when there was this beautiful canyon, knee deep in grass? Why not establish a ranch here, on the Apishapa?

Goodnight set his crew to building a log cabin. He put the tired steers out on the grass. The rocky walls boxed them in nicely, so two riders could handle them. Then Goodnight went back to Texas, joined Loving's son, Joe, with another herd of four thousand, and ran the Comanche gauntlet again. After many skirmishes, the two finally straggled in to the new ranch with thirty-two hundred head.

In spite of the cold, the herd wintered well. In the spring a prominent Denver cattleman, John Iliff, to whom Loving had sold cattle the year before, came to the ranch. He laid out forty thousand dollars in gold certificates for the fat steers. Some he would drive to the Union Pacific railroad for shipment to Chicago slaughterhouses. The remainder he would trail to Cheyenne, Wyoming, where they would be sold to young men opening up ranches on the northern plains.

In three years Goodnight delivered thirty thousand cattle to the Colorado market. Many of the rangy beeves fed miners, settlers and railroad workers, while as many more were bought by frontiering landholders to stock the northern ranges of Colorado and Wyoming. The supply of cattle Goodnight and other Texans delivered to New Mexico kept the reservation-bound Indians fairly content, and helped establish cattle raising as a prime industry on land that was, before irrigation, ninety-eight precent unfit for crop production. For over twenty years cattle moved out of Texas over the Goodnight-Loving trail. In time the Comanches were whipped, and there was no more bloodshed. Then the old trail succumbed to the press of people along its flanks. Barbed wire appeared around the water holes. Small-scale ranchers, contemptuously called nesters, broke up the far-flung free open range. The introduction of blooded shorthorn stock altered the appearance and character of the Longhorns, and finally the old thoroughfare was rubbed out by crops and concrete highways.

8

Chisholm Trail

Texas to Kansas

Not all Kansans feared the tick-laden Longhorns. The cattle buyers and feeders who needed Texas beeves to expand their business didn't, nor did the slaughterhouse operators. Also, railroads racing each other across Kansas could use the freight hauling. All were alert to the loopholes in the law. The trouble was, there was no new trail outside the quarantine area, nor a market west of Kansas City.

Fortunately there was a man like Joseph G. McCoy ready to take action. The twenty-nine-year-old McCoy, a tall bluff man with a loud voice, had been raised on a farm in Illinois near where neighbors had fattened Texas cattle before the war. With his two brothers, he had bought, fattened, and shipped mules, hogs, sheep, and cattle from New Orleans to Chicago and New York. He knew the business. As he saw it, the problem was to find a place where the drovers could bring their Longhorns without being attacked, and where buyers could ship easily to feeders and packers.

McCoy took a Missouri Pacific train from St. Louis to Kansas City, which he described as an "unsightly aggregation of bluffs and almost canyon-like gorges, bisected with deep cuts and large fills called streets." All along steep Main Street, he asked questions about the livestock business. Then he went further west to Abilene. The little frontier town then boasted about twelve dirt-roofed cabins, a six-room hotel, a blacksmith shop, the Frontier Store, a saloon, and nearby a stage station. Here McCoy paid a dollar for a miserable meal "of strong black coffee, strips of pork fat fried to a sandy crispness, and half-baked soggy indigestible biscuits." There was plenty of room for stockyards at Abilene, but unfortunately the town was sixty miles inside the barrier line established by the quarantine law. Nevertheless McCoy took a chance. He bought 250 acres and ordered lumber hauled in. By September first he had a shipping yard that would handle one thousand cattle. He also added a big scale, a barn, an office, a livery stable, and a $15,000 eighty-guest hotel which he named the Drover's Cottage.

McCoy had handbills printed which advertised his marketing center. These were distributed throughout the southwest. He also sent a rider to intercept the herds on the trail, and persuade their drovers to go west and north to Abilene. The Texans listened to the messenger. It all sounded too good to be true. But even if there was a catch in it somewhere, they were desperate enough to give Abilene a chance. They turned their beeves toward McCoy's new plant. Much of the way was blazed, thanks to two men. One is now forgotten; the other was made famous when his name was given to this new trail between Texas and Abilene, the Chisholm Trail.

Wayne Gard, an authority on the Chisholm Trail, traces it in an almost straight line from the Rio Grande river on the south to Abilene on the north. The cattle were rounded up and the marketable steers were thrown onto the trail from many areas throughout central Texas. Some joined feeder trails east of San Antonio and went north to Austin. Here other feeders came in as the line went north to Waco. At Waco the old Texas Road (also called the

Shawnee Trail) lined out to Dallas, but the Chisholm Trail paralleled it for a few miles and then gradually pulled further west past Fort Worth. The herds crossed the Red River at Red River Station, which was about 125 miles west of the long-used crossing on the Texas Road. Then the Chisholm Trail went due north on a segment on which Buffalo Bill Matthewson, a famous buffalo hunter now long forgotten, broke the original trail up to the Washita River, and thence on northward to Jesse Chisholm's trading post on the North Canadian River.

Chisholm, a much-respected man, had started out as a packhorse Indian trader, and had opened a little post. Later he blazed a wagon route north from there, and opened a new post and ranch near the present site of Wichita, Kansas. He never referred to his "road" as the Chisholm Trail. In his mind, it was just a wagon road. Once across the North Canadian River, the cattle drovers need only follow his wagon tracks to Wichita. After swimming the Arkansas River, the herds grazed aimlessly while the trail bosses sought the best way into Abilene. When McCoy learned of this difficulty, he sent a surveyor to mark a road on this last segment of the long haul up from Texas. The surveyor used mounds of dirt as markers, and topped each one with a Lone Star Flag.

Even though Chisholm had opened only the middle portion of the trail, his name was given to the entire route. Today the Chisholm Trail is well remembered as perhaps the greatest cattle trail in American history. Certainly more cattle, an estimated ten million, moved over it than any other trail. Jesse Chisholm did not trail cattle on it, nor did he know Joseph McCoy.

Even before the last nail had been driven in McCoy's pens and chutes, there were over seven thousand cattle awaiting shipment. The first herd to reach Abilene belonged to three men named Smith,

McCord, and Chandler. McCoy bought their beeves. He wrote, "Due to the incessant rains and the grass turning soft, their cattle were in poor condition. But I offered them a fair price which they accepted. Two days later they drove into the newly-finished shipping pens."

But the cattle did not come in as fast as McCoy had hoped. He wrote later, " They [the Texans] were not ready to credit the proposition that the day of fair dealing had dawned for Texas drovers, and the era of mobs, brutal murder, and arbitrary prescription had ended forever." Still, the first shipment of twenty cars left Abilene on September 5, 1867, for Chicago. There was a big celebration that night in the as-yet uncompleted hotel. McCoy was the hero of the hour. He had opened a new era in the cattle business.

In the next four months more than thirty thousand cattle arrived, and one thousand cattle cars rattled eastward to market. Satisfied drovers and owners passed the word down the trail that they had

been well treated at Abilene, and what was equally important, had run into no unusual difficulties on the Chisholm Trail.

Of course there had to be some trouble. The farmers in the Abilene area held a protest meeting. "By gum, we're not havin' those fever-carriers near our farms. We'll stampede 'em!" they threatened. McCoy had the courage to attend their meeting. He faced them down. He talked in glowing terms of how his new business would make the area grow, and increase the value of their land. Then the Texas trail bosses who had come to the meeting with him said they would buy the farmers' butter, eggs, potatoes, onions, corn, oats, and hay, and not quibble at the prices.

As soon as the farmers realized they might profit from the cattlemen, they decided they could afford to let the Longhorns pass. There was no further trouble. The glowing picture McCoy had painted came true in 1868. Some 75,000 cattle poured into Abilene. True, they chewed the free grass for miles around, and roiled the Smoky

Hill River. But the trail bosses made big purchases of farm products, and the cowboys squandered their wages in the saloons and dance halls that sprung up along Abilene's main street. The cattle and the cowboys brought an undreamed-of prosperity to the little shack town.

Maybe it was too good to be true. By July reports were filtering back from the east of a dreadful outbreak of Texas fever. Illinois banned Texas cattle. So did New York, where fine herds of purebred livestock were now well established. The sales cut off sharply in Abilene, and the year that had started on such high hopes dwindled out.

Things were better in 1869. Several states had passed laws forbidding the entry of Texas cattle unless they had been wintered in the north, and were supposedly free of the fever. What the drovers needed now were affadavits swearing that their cattle had been wintered in the north, or at least in Kansas, Iowa or Wisconsin. There were enough corrupt officials who could be bribed into issuing such papers, so once more Texas cattle were in demand, and rattled off in cattle cars. This time they went in three directions: east, west over the Union Pacific railroad into Colorado and Utah, and north overland as far as Wyoming and Montana. Oddly enough, there was little trouble from Texas fever that year.

Most of the trail bosses made money. Randolph Paine of Denton County, Texas bought 3,000 steers at twelve dollars a head, shaped up a herd, pushed it north through good grass, and sold his steers at thirty dollars apiece in Abilene. Others weren't so lucky. Either they lost men and cattle crossing swollen rivers, ran into storms, suffered stampedes, or had to pay damages when their herds overran small settlements. Still, 300,000 cattle went through the Abilene yards, and 2,000 carloads were shipped east.

With rival towns such as Junction City, Wichita, and Newton, Kansas linked with railroads and offering sales markets, the Texans put 600,000 head up the Chisholm Trail in 1871. In the late summer the market prices began to fall, and when winter came on, there were 300,000 unsold cattle in the Abilene area alone. The drovers were hard-pressed to find grass enough so they could hold their herds until the market improved. Then even this scarce grass vanished in the wake of a wind-driven prairie fire. Afterwards the thin-hided Texas cattle bawled for feed. There was no grass, and no hay, and it was getting colder. They huddled in shallow draws, trying vainly to escape the wind. One day it began to rain, a cold slashing rain that soon turned to sleet, then ice, and howled out in a terrible blizzard. The Texas critters froze in their tracks. When spring came, the prairie was strewn with their stinking carcasses. Skinners went out to retrieve the hides, and got over 50,000 of them. Quite a few cattlemen lost fortunes in that awful winter die-up. But it didn't stop them. They hoped to recoup their fortunes in 1872.

Meantime Abilene had changed. New people had come in with the prosperity McCoy had brought to the little town. But many of these newcomers were farmers, who thoroughly disapproved of the wild goings on when the rowdy cowboys hit town. So, with other towns vying for this "disreputable" trade, the good people of Abilene told the cattlemen to take their business somewhere else. They did. Poor Joseph McCoy lost most of his money with the decline of the trade, and was forced to sell his stockyards at a great loss.

The picture was changing; even the cattle themselves were no longer the same. The day was long past when a man with a rope and branding iron could build a herd from wild cattle. A few still roamed the thickets, but most had been branded and brought into semi-domesticated herds. And now that they had time to observe and think about it, the foresighted Texas cattlemen looked at their long-legged critters and were dissatisfied with them. Longhorns took eight to ten years to mature, and even then, never were much for putting on weight. So the Texans in the northwestern part of the state began importing, from the north, meaty shorthorns, Durhams, to upgrade their herds. At first a good many succumbed to tick fever, but enough survived to produce fever-resistant stock. By 1872, Joseph McCoy wrote that the steers coming into Wichita, where he had moved from Abilene, were younger, stockier, beefier, and their horns were not as long.

In 1872, Texas was well on its way toward recovering from the postwar slump. Railroads had come in, and tied Texas in to the rest of the nation. In a few places, packing plants were canning beef successfully for shipment. Even new-fangled refrigerator cars were transporting fresh meat northward. Many cattlemen found a good market only a few miles from their ranches. They did not have to leave the state.

Gradually traffic on the Chisholm Trail beyond the Red River slackened. Actually, the great days of the trail were over. Wherever the cattlemen had gone, others came in their wake—mostly farmers. They fenced off the free grass. After barbed wire was introduced in 1874, they strung it across the trail in many places. They also did not want their herds coming into contact with the tick-infested Longhorns. So in area after area along the great trail, once more citizens and farmers took up rifles and pitchforks and turned back the Texas stock.

The traffic trickled on until 1885. Then the dust settled, and sustained traffic on the Chisholm Trail was a thing of the past.

But there were still hundreds of thousands of Longhorns ready for market, and Texans willing to face the great hardships to get them there. So they sought another trail, and in time found a new one, another wild town that welcomed them, and a new market at Dodge City, Kansas.

9

The Western Trail

Texas to Kansas

In May of 1877, two cattlemen named Maxwell and Morris contracted to deliver two thousand head from southern Texas to Ogallala, Nebraska. When they discussed the difficulties sure to lie ahead, they decided to make a big gamble: they would avoid the Chisholm Trail and blaze a new one further west.

"We'll be going through unsettled country, and there's no maps to guide us," Maxwell reminded his partner.

Morris shrugged. "The North Star is all the compass we need."

From Belton, Texas, the two struck northwest and followed the Leon River through present-day Coryell, Hamilton, Comanche, Eastland, and Stephens counties. Finally they stumbled onto Fort Griffin, a military outpost and buffalo hunters' town, west of Fort Worth. The cattle sniffed the rank odor of the buffalo hides, and stampeded. Maxwell and Morris spent a day and a half a night rounding them up, and getting them settled on the grass several miles from town. Then they pointed north over unmarked brush-covered wilderness. The cattle persistently tried to hide in the thickets. The crew had to shout, fire guns, and spin ropes to keep them moving.

As soon as the Red River was sighted, the herd was held back while Maxwell rode to the river bank. Because the spring rains had been light, the muddy stream was still in its meandering, narrow channel. Sand flats gave easy access from the bank to the water.

"It looks too good to be true," Maxwell commented, thumbing back his hat and relaxing a moment in the saddle.

Morris grunted. He knew Texas rivers. He spurred his horse and rode onto the sand. His horse immediately began to flounder. He spurred the animal, turned him hard, and rode back to solid ground. "Quicksand," he said disgustedly.

That was expected. And it was not an insurmountable problem, if the herd was put to running, and hit the sand with enough speed to keep it moving across and onto the far bank. The two told the crew the bad news. Maxwell and one man stayed out front while Morris contacted the drag riders. They dismounted and tightened their saddle cinches. When Morris circled the drag, he hauled out his pistol and waved to his partner. Up front Maxwell hollered, fired his gun in the air, and waved. The cattle tossed their horns, bawled in fright, and began to run. At the sides and rear, the cowboys kept shouting and spinning their ropes. The lead animals pounded onto the sand, floundered a little, but being pressed from behind by others, and being spooked, they plunged on across the sandflats and river to the far shore. Here Maxwell and his helper got them to circling. Before long all had slowed to a stop, and were grazing on the thick grass.

An easy crossing was cause for celebration. There still were countless creeks and other rivers ahead. Fortunately, because they were angling northwest now, and far upstream, they had no trouble walking the herd across the Washita, the Canadian, the North Canadian and even the Cimarron rivers. The partners congratulated them-

selves on their good luck. For the most part the route they were blazing lay across open country, with easy stream crossings and no timber. And they hadn't seen a piece of barbed wire the entire distance. Discounting the expected annoyances, the trip so far had been unusually good. But good luck has a way of changing.

One evening after the cattle had been watered, and were grazing quietly before bedding down, the wind began to pick up. A black cloud slowly engulfed the starbright sky. It began to rain. Thunder rolled and crashed, and jagged flashes of lightning split the sky and hammered the ground. The horns of the cattle seemed tipped with fire. They wanted to run, but didn't know which way to go, so they began milling and bawling. The riders trod back and forth, shouting and firing their guns to keep them circling. Time and time again a bolt exploded amidst the frightened cattle. The riders spent an exhausting night holding the herd. Even after the storm passed, the air smelled of sulphur and the cattle would not quiet down. At the first streak of dawn, when the cook started a fire with the dry kindling he

always carried in a sling under the wagon, the partners tallied the damage. Lightning had killed seven head, and the herd obviously had run off some of the weight put on during the overland trek.

But at least there were no Kiowas or Comanches bothering them. The northward drive continued. Several nights later a peculiar stillness was in the air, and the distinctive smell of sulphur spelled trouble. As a precaution, Maxwell had the chuckwagon roped down, in case a bad wind developed. He also removed his pistol and spurs and tucked them in his bedroll. The crew followed suit because they believed that steel attracted lightning. Soon a torrential rain and heavy wind hit the camp broadside. Chain lightning flashed continuously. Again the cattle bawled and milled, and again every man spent a miserable night. At the peak of the crashing and hammering, a bolt of lightning hit the steel shoe on the wagon pole, and struck a cowboy riding twenty feet away, killing him and his horse. In the morning, when the crew sorrowfully buried him, they removed his gold watch to send to his family. The bolt had melted it into a shapeless mass of gold and splintered glass.

Fortunately no further storms plagued the drive. When the owners came onto the military road, which they knew ran from Camp Supply to the south of them all the way to Fort Dodge on the north, they turned onto it. Ruts and campsites marked the way to the Arkansas River. Here the partners held the herd on the good grass covering the river bottomland, while they rode into Dodge City and viewed the shipping pens alongside the railroad.

Maxwell and Morris found Dodge City in the doldrums. The multi-million buffalo herd had been shot out of existence, and there was no business. A few hunters and skinners still idled about town, but most had deserted the once-rambunctious burg. The two men learned something important. If given ample notice, cattle buyers from eastern Kansas would ride the train to Dodge City, and be on hand next season to buy any Texas herds that appeared. In other words, Dodge City welcomed cattle. No one was apt to be fussy about tick fever or the quarantine law. So Maxwell and Morris moved their cattle on to Nebraska, as they had contracted, and then carried the good news back to Texas. It circulated widely during the winter months. Once more cattlemen took heart. A road to the north, free of barbed wire and armed troublemakers, with good grass and few tough passages, and a guaranteed market at a railhead!

"Reckon that new western trail is worth a try?" they asked one another, inadvertently giving the trail a name that would stick.

Try the Western Trail they did, to the tune of a quarter of a million cattle in 1878.

When Jonathan Doan brought two wagon loads of merchandise to the banks of the Red River where Maxwell and Morris had crossed earlier (at a point 25 miles north of present-day Vernon, Texas) he provided a much-needed frontier supply point. At first

Doan operated from a brush wickiup with a canvas sheet for a front door. But soon he had an adobe structure built, and then he replaced this with a rectangular frame building. Thousands upon thousands of cattle grazed the grass for miles around his store, while waiting to cross the Red River's quicksands. Seeing this as an additional source of revenue. Doan set a crew to cutting brush and grass to form a springy bridge over the quicksand. It worked, and many cattlemen gladly paid a toll of twenty-five cents a head to avoid the dangerous, sucking ground. Doan's Crossing was also the gathering place for stockmen to swap information. In time the store boasted a post-office, so men on the trail could keep in touch with wives and sweet-hearts before pushing on into the unsettled country.

But, as happened before whenever Texas stockmen opened up new country, settlers followed in their wake. Mostly they were small operators. When they strung barbed wire around the precious and far-spaced water holes, a shooting war broke out between the new-comers and the trail drivers. But if the barbed wire was cut, it tangled in the horns and tails of the cattle, and made them stampede. The farmers rushed out with guns leveled, and set their dogs on the herd. The cowboys shot the dogs. The farmers fumed, but were powerless. The herds got to the water, and after quieting down, passed on. Nevertheless the cattlemen knew this was a sign of what the future held, when more and more farmers moved in.

The next year when the herds reached the Red River, it was in flood. While the stockmen held their cattle back, waiting for the water to subside, a stranger appeared. He said he was an "inspec-tor." He said he had authority from the state to inspect every head of cattle for proper ownership, and would charge ten cents a head for the service. The trail drivers could not proceed across the river without paying for this "certificate of inspection."

The cattlemen talked it over, and pretended to agree to the inspection. The next morning they invited the phony inspector to have breakfast with them. The greedy man accepted the invitation. But he found himself jumped on, tied up, and tossed into a plum thicket, where he lay bruised, scratched, and very much at the mercy of gnats and mosquitoes. The trail bosses crossed their herds without procuring any certificates, and the crook finally was rescued by his friends.

But these were minor troubles. The cattle and mustangs poured up the Western Trail, a quarter of a million head each year until 1885. But there was a difference. Although thousands were shipped from Dodge City east to St. Louis and Chicago, or to Kansas slaughterhouses, the bulk of the herds was trailed on into Nebraska, Wyoming, and Montana. In other words, they were not directed to meat markets, but to form the basis of the great herds that would soon supplant the buffalo on the sun-cured grass of the northern ranges. The new ranchers in the Sioux and Crow country imported Durham shorthorns to upgrade their Texas beef. This, coupled with the efforts the Texans had been making to upgrade their herds in the same manner, spelled doom for the long-legged, half-wild spooky Texas stock. In their place there developed a more manageable, meatier, younger-maturing beef that ultimately brought a better price on the market, and thus benefited cattlemen and consumers alike.

Yes, times were changing. Only the old-timers talked about Indian raids, and trailing weeks on end without crossing a settler's path. Wages were better, too. A cowhand might earn forty dollars a month and grub for his round-the-clock, no-Sundays-off job, but he still had to furnish his horse and equipment.

The Western Trail narrowed as more and more settlers came onto the plains. Soon the Texans encountered mile upon mile cross-hatched with barbed wire. Sometimes they had to pay to get at water and grass. Other times, they faced drawn guns, and moved on. In 1885, a statewide embargo in Kansas against tick-laden cattle went into effect. The spread of arms and fenced pastures across southern Kansas cut off the middle portion of the trail, and halted all traffic. Shipping cattle from Dodge City trickled to nothing.

But some Texans were a stubborn lot. They would not give up trail driving. They insisted on moving their herds overland, even though throughout Texas shipping cattle north by railroad was now the easier, if the more costly way of operating. So, throughout 1883 and 1884 and 1885, these cattlemen besieged Congress with demands for the establishment of a so-called National Trail. They asked that a route be laid across government-owned land where they would not be plagued by toll-taking Indians, or barbed-wire fences, or tick-shy farmers. They urged that such a trail extend from the Red River all the way to the Canadian boundary, using the Western Trail and extensions through Nebraska and the Dakotas. The cattlemen even agreed to pay to use the trail, so there would be money available to maintain and guard the trail's boundaries. But they argued in vain. Congress turned a deaf ear to the proposal.

So, trail driving north from Texas gradually petered out. The hard-beaten, over-grazed earth basked under sun and rain. In a few seasons the grass came back, and wiped out all sign of the great northbound drive.

But the final chapters of America's cattle trails had not yet been written.

10

No Place For Weaklings

Trailing cattle at any time, from the days of Coronado to the great Texas drives, was dangerous work. There was no place for weaklings. What about the trail bosses and cowboys? What manner of men were they? How did they carry on their difficult work?

Take the trail bosses, the professional trail drivers. Mostly they were men in their late twenties. They had to be a combination of intelligent businessman and saddle-smart cowboy. They had to know cattle, their habits and menace. They had to be gamblers in the sense that they gambled on buying a herd at one price, and on pushing it to market despite all manner of trouble and danger, and on selling it at a higher price to make a profit. They had to be leaders, of even temper, and know the land ahead. Many were veterans of several drives north before they took on the risk of bossing a herd.

As one old-time boss described his work, "He must see that there are enough provisions, as short grub does more toward dissatisfying the cowboy than anything else. He must assign each man to his proper duty. He must ride ahead to see that there is water at the proper distance. He must know when and where to stop for noon.

He must count the cattle at intervals to see that none have been lost. He must settle all difficulties between his men."

Another said, "A good boss rides about three or four times as far as the herd goes." He never pushed his Longhorns too hard, and never let them suspect they were being pushed. He remembered the old saying, "Look out for the cows' feet and the horses' backs, and let the cowboys and cook look out for themselves."

Usually a trail driver contracted with various ranchers for the cattle they wished to sell. These were counted, and a price agreed upon. He did not pay for the cattle then, but agreed on the price he would pay after the cattle were sold. Thus every head he lost on the trail cut down on his profits. Since these cattle belonged to several ranchers, they bore different brands. In order to keep track of them on the road, the trail boss had his crew brand them with his brand. This was called the road brand. When the separate bunches of cattle were brought together, run through a chute, and branded, they were "shaped up," or rounded up, and "thrown" on the trail.

A trail herd numbered from a few hundred to several thousand head. They were of two types: mature steers, or beeves, or mixed herds of steers, cows, and yearlings. The beeves were sold for marketing to slaughterhouses, the mixed herds for stocking northern ranges. Calves born during the drive were killed because they were a drag on the cows, and slowed the pace of some ten to fifteen miles daily.

The first days on the road were the most critical. Usually the herd was driven very hard for the first two or three days, so it would not want to double back, or scatter. Once used to moving ahead, the beeves dropped into line, and usually kept their places. The leaders showed themselves by moving up front, and asserting their position. Then all the trail boss had to do was move the cattle, valued at from ten to fifty thousand dollars, to market. To do this he had to withstand the losses from stampedes, drowning, Indian raids and sickness, sell at the best price possible, pay off the crew, pay off the ranchers, and hope to have some money left over for several months' round-the-clock work. If the market price in Kansas was down, he might have had to hold his herd on the grass for several months until the price improved. If the price worsened, he might have had to drive his cattle elsewhere, or sell at a loss.

Take young Sol West, a Texan. He headed north with a thousand head. He lost several swimming swollen rivers. Indians demanded toll more than once. He ran into a blizzard. Temperatures plummeted so low that many of this cowboys' horses froze to death. His cattle reached Kansas in such poor condition that he had to keep them on grass two months before they were fit to be sold. They didn't bring a good price. When he got home, paid for the cattle, and paid off the crew and the storekeeper for supplies, he had $1.50 to show for six months' hard work. But Sol was one of the unluckier ones. Some men made thousands of dollars in profits from trail driving. A few even became wealthy.

After pocketing the large sum of cash from the sale, the trail boss usually paid his crew. They had a couple of days of fun—whooping it up, dancing, and losing most of their pay to gamblers—and then were ready to head for home. To thwart outlaws who preyed on travelers, they slipped out of town secretly and rode at night to outpace them and any unfriendly Indians lurking about. With luck the cowboys arrived home all in one piece. In spite of all these troubles, there never was a lack of good trail drivers in the business. If they had a profitable trip or two, many went into ranching on their own. At first they drove their own herds north, and then, if luck still was with them and they made money, they turned the hard work over to other young trail bosses.

What about the trail boss's crew, the cowboys? Most were young lads in their teens and early twenties. Some were sons of stock raisers; some were drifters; many were greenhorns who had never chalked up a trip to their credit. If a lad had made two or three trips, was dependable, loyal, courageous, and a hard worker, he was considered a "top hand." If he had made four or more trips, he was an old veteran. A few made a career of trail driving, but many either went into cattle raising, or left the business forever. Mostly they were young Americans, sons of pioneering settlers, though there were a few English adventurers, some Mexican *vaqueros*, Negro drovers, and Chinese "waddies."

Personal loyalty to a trail boss wasn't enough. Trailing cattle promised a long haul accompanied by dirt, fatigue, danger, monotony, and long weeks with the same men, sleeping on the ground, and eating plain food. Some couldn't take it, and quit, leaving the crew short-handed. Others grumbled the whole way and couldn't wait for pay day, and that day never came until after the herd was sold. In the early days the pay was poor—fifteen to thirty dollars a month and grub, with the cowboy furnishing his own horse, saddle, ropes, blankets, and guns. They had to put up with heat, cold, dust, sweat-burn, saddle gall, insects, skunks, rattlesnakes, wolves and bears, swollen streams, ornery cow horses, storms, lightning, stampedes, Indian raids, rustlers, and irate settlers.

The cowboy had to work as part of a closely-knit team; be neither coward nor bully, neither overbearing nor subservient. He had to be suspicious of cattle, because the ornery dumb critters couldn't be trusted five minutes. He had to be able to make a snap judgment that put neither himself nor the cattle in jeopardy. He had to be "long on memory," spotting troublesome beeves or trouble spots on the trail. He had to withstand quick changes in temperatures, the onslaught of storms, quicksand, poisonous weeds and water and flash floods. He had to keep awake day and night, if need be, and spend long, monotonous hours in the saddle, knowing that calm could explode in a second because a steer took a notion to bolt. Once the herd started to run, he had to stay with it, racing in the dark over rough country pocked with holes or deep cuts.

And yet, despite this catalogue of woes, hundreds of boys every season clamored to join an outfit and head north. The job spelled excitement and adventure, and a chance to cut away from home and see the country; to wear boots, swing a rope, eat chuckwagon fare, ride and ride and ride, and cut a caper in a cowtown at the end of the trail.

Though the cowboy is a distinct American type, he inherited a large part of his equipment, methods, and language from the Spanish and Mexican cattlemen of the very early days. His clothes were designed for the job at hand, and a far cry from those worn by movie and television cowboys. First, the hat. It was broad-brimmed to protect a cowboy's neck and head and eyes from the blazing sun. It served as an umbrella in the rain. The crown made a handy water bucket if a cowboy's horse was unable to get water. The brim served as a drinking cup. A cowboy started his campfire by using his hat as a bellows to fan a weak blaze. It was also used for signaling. In cold weather, the brim was pulled down and tied with a handkerchief to protect his ears.

Trousers had to be narrow, and of rugged cotton material to withstand the hard work and riding. Where there was heavy underbrush, leather chaps were slipped on to protect the legs and thighs. Most cowboys wore galluses, or suspenders, because a belt often cut a man seated on a saddle.

A neckerchief was indispensable. It was used to cover nose and mouth from heavy dust or freezing sleet, to tie down a hat, as a towel, mop, bronc blindfold, hobble, sling, tourniquet, bandage, and signal marker, but seldom to wipe a man's nose! For everyday use, the kerchief was grey, blue, or blue and red print. When a cowboy got to town and spruced up, he usually blossomed out in a bright red or yellow silk one.

Because pants' pockets were unhandy for a man in the saddle, cowboys used vests of leather or heavy sailcloth. These had four small pockets in them, for holding "makings," cigarette tobacco and rice papers and matches, or snuff, or chewing tobacco. Cowboys disliked "tailor mades," or factory-rolled cigarettes, because they crushed too easily. Shirts were usually collarless, of grey or blue cotton or wool, with elastic arm-bands holding the cuffs at their proper place.

Two-inch heels on boots were not for show. The high heel was worn to give the cowboy protection against losing his stirrups at critical moments. Since the heel extended below the stirrup, it kept the boot from slipping through, when a cowboy applied sudden pressure on quick stops or turns. The soft leather top of the boot, almost knee high, protected ankles and calves against wear and tear and rattlesnakes. It was broad enough so the pants could be tucked into it, thus preventing snags on brush. Nickel-plated spurs were worn with them. However, the high-heeled boots had one disadvantage; they were very uncomfortable for walking. A cowboy seldom walked a block, if he had to.

Cowboy underwear came in two styles: the long-handled red flannel variety, or three-quarter-length cotton union suits. Socks were grey, but mostly black. A cowboy always had a raincoat or slicker, which he kept handy at all times by tying it behind his saddle.

The cowboy's outfit also consisted of his high pommeled saddle,

a revolver or two, a bedroll, and a lariat. The lariat had many uses. A cowboy used it to catch his horse, drag wood to camp, pull cattle from bogholes, throw an ornery steer, or pull the wagon across streams. An extra length came in handy for tying up a bedroll, staking out a horse, lining out a corral, killing snakes, and whipping cows in line.

Every cowboy had a horse, but this mount was turned into the horse herd on the trail drive. The boss had to furnish from three to eight horses for each cowboy to use on the road. These were mostly mature, hardy cow ponies that could stand long hours, hard work, and considerable abuse. Although he might treat his own horse well, a cowboy had little regard for the cayuses furnished for his work.

Horses were cheap and expendable in Texas, and cowboys used them with little consideration. Most were sold at the end of the drive. A cowboy soon noted which horse was the most sure-footed and sharp-eyed, and used that mount for night herding. Horses were changed at morning, noon, and dinner time, and again for night riding. Most were of mustang blood, and only a generation or two removed from the wild horses of Spanish breed that had roamed Texas.

The most experienced and dependable cowboys rode "point." These "pointers" rode near the head of the herd, one on each side, and guided the lead steers. They controlled both the direction and speed at which the herd moved. Theirs was the most responsible position. They were the first to ford rivers, or to meet a frontal attack from rustlers.

Next came the "swings." These two men rode on opposite sides of the thin line of cattle, about one third of the way back from the point. They helped keep the pace, and hold the cattle in line. Another third of the way back rode the "flankers" who kept the line moving and the strays from straggling. The most disagreeable task and position was that of the "drag" riders in the rear. They ate dust all day and had to keep the lazy or perverse animals moving. The newest, greenest boys were the drag riders.

The wrangler was the low man in the outfit. Usually he was a young lad, or an older cowboy too crippled to ride herd. The wrangler had to round up the horses at dawn so the riders could rope their day mounts, trail them to the midday stop, cut out fresh horses for the riders, trail again to the night stop, cut out the night horses, eat, and then put the horses out to graze, and sleep near them.

A cowboy didn't know the meaning of an eight-hour day. He rose at dawn, shook down his clothing, pulled on his boots and hat, and dashed cold water on his gritty face. He seldom bothered to shave or brush his teeth. Then he tore into a breakfast of hot cakes swimming in syrup, bacon or salt pork, and sourdough biscuits with jam. Some mornings he was treated to fried potatoes, cooked cereal, stewed fruit, and thin, tough, fried-to-a-turn beef or venison steak. Cowboys liked their coffee very strong. An old-time cook said the recipe was "Take two pounds of Arbuckle's coffee, put in enough water to wet it down, boil it four hours, and then toss in a hoss shoe. If the hoss shoe sinks, the coffee ain't ready."

A good cook made for a satisfied crew, and if he could bandage cuts and set broken bones, and dose fevers, all the better. The constant changes in water usually gave the men dysentery. The cook remedied this by brewing up a strong tea of snakeroot, or the inside bark of a cottonwood tree. A seriously-ill or injured cowboy created a crisis. No men could be spared to ride with him to the nearest town or ranch. The best he could hope for, one old-timer said, was to make a speedy recovery, or die as quickly as possible.

After eating, the cowboy rolled up his bed and dumped it on the ground next to the cook's wagon. Then he selected his horse from the "cavvy" brought in by the young wrangler. Once saddled and mounted, he started pushing the cattle easily onto the trail. Meantime the cook and his helper, if he had one, cleaned the pots and dishes, packed the food, stowed the gear and bedrolls in the wagon, and hitched horses or mules to it. Then the cook passed the herd, and went on to the spot designated by the trail boss for the noon stop, and got the next meal under way. The wrangler rounded up the horses, drove them past the herd, and grazed them not far from the cook wagon at noon and night.

During the early morning hours the cattle grazed along the trail, then were driven steadily for three or four miles, to a watering place if possible. After drinking, they were allowed to lie down and rest during the heat of the day. June, July and August temperatures were usually in the nineties, and often reached one hundred degrees. Cattle could not be driven then because they would sicken, and lose weight rapidly. After a light lunch, the cowboys enjoyed a smoke, sometimes a quick snooze, and then saddled another horse for the afternoon drive.

When the worst heat of the day was over, the herd began getting to its feet and grazed until late afternoon. Then it was pushed along the trail for seven or eight miles. Meantime the boss had ridden ahead and chosen the night camp spot, near good water and grass.

The cook arrived, unhitched and unpacked, and started dinner. Usually he served more sourdough biscuits, steak and coffee, and dried beans that had soaked overnight and cooked long over a slow fire. The cowboys called them "prairie strawberries." Sometimes the cook offered canned tomatoes and pickles, a great treat. The cowboys liked stew, but if they could tell what was in it, it wasn't a good stew! As one cowboy said, "You throw everything in the pot but the horns, hair and holler. And the longer it cooks, the better." Dessert could be one of three dishes: dried apple or raisin pie, "lick" or biscuits topped with molassses, or "boggy top," cooked dried fruit baked with a biscuit topping. The men ate with their hats on, sitting cross-legged on the ground. Afterwards, they dropped their tin plates and cutlery in a dishpan filled with hot soapy water, which they called the "wreck pan."

The cattle grazed until dusk, and then were rounded up on the bed ground, usually an open, fairly level place away from timber and gulleys. On a strange route never traveled before, or during cloudy weather, the trail boss had the cook point the wagon tongue in line with the North Star so that in the morning the herd would be headed in the right direction.

Every member of the crew, except the cook and night wrangler, took his turn at night guard duty, two or three men to each two-hour shift. The best, sure-footed horses were used. Most stampedes occurred at night, so the cowboy's life depended on the skill a horse had to run, dodge, keep his footing, and pick his way through inky darkness.

While riding around the herd, many cowboys sang to the animals at night. This not only reassured the spooky cattle, but it kept the cowboy awake. No matter that he might have a voice like a coyote. He never struck a match, or made an unusual sound because that could make a brute jump to his feet, bawl, and churn up a run. The cowboy told time by the stars, and soon learned to know when his two hours were up, and it was time to ride toward the fire, waken his relief man, drink some coffee, and then flop into his bedroll. He always slept with his clothes on, except his boots and hat. His night horse was tethered at his side, or nearby.

The herd was seldom quiet for long at night. Some animals would sleep a while, then rise and stretch, graze a bit, and lie down again. They had to be watched carefully to see they didn't wander off. A herd often drifted a mile or two during the night. It was up to the night guard to keep this movement under control. The period of greatest danger was from midnight to two in the morning, because after sleeping the first part of the night on one side, the cattle would

rise, mill a little, and then if not alarmed, would lie down on the other side for some two hours.

The threat of a stampede was always present, but it happened more often at night. The sudden bark of a coyote, a horse's shoe ringing against a rock, a flash of lightning, a loud voice, or a thousand other things, could bring a quiet herd to its feet and running wildly in the dark. The awful bellowing, the clatter of the horns, the earth shaking as thousands of hooves pounded, created a nightmare. Cowboys had to follow alongside the fear-crazed critters. The pointers up front were in the greatest danger. They had to keep from being trampled, and also try to turn the frightened leaders. Once the point, or lead, was turned, the herd would circle and bawl and mill, but gradually settle down. The trouble was, the steers would remain jumpy for days, and be inclined to stampede again and again.

At dawn the exhausted riders would put the cattle back on the trail and "squeeze 'em down" into a slow-moving line, so they could be counted. Sometimes one, or a hundred, would be missing, so riders would be sent out in all directions to gather them in.

There was a lot of monotony in driving cattle sixty to seventy days on the trail. It was very wearing on tempers: the hours of eating dust, hearing the rumble of hoofs and clatter of horns, breathing the nauseating smell of sweating cattle, perspiring under a hammer-hot sun, freezing in the face of a northern wind, being soaked in a cold rain, . . . all these made for aches and pains and bruises and fatigue and short tempers that took the "romance" out of the drive. But there usually was time, before hitting the bedrolls, to swap yarns while seated around a cheerful fire, and listen to a cowboy's fiddle or harmonica. In spite of the danger and hardships, there must have been a strong pull in trail driving, because no herd ever went north without a full crew of eager, young Americans.

11

California

Cattle came late to California. Spanish galleons touched the coast of southern California as early as 1542, and at different times and places thereafter. However, the first herd was not trailed into the region until 1769 when Gaspar de Portola, Governor of Lower California, and Father Junipero Serra of the Franciscan order led a colonizing expedition to San Diego. At the mission established there, the local Indians were converted to Christianity, and taught how to cultivate gardens and vineyards, tan hides, and handle cattle. Thanks to the abundance of sunshine, good grass, and water, the herd did well. As twenty more missions were founded, each a day's ride from one another as far north as present-day Sonoma, they were stocked with "18 head of horned cattle" and other livestock from the San Diego mission. From this first four hundred head, and others that trekked in small herds overland from Mexico, the number swelled unbelievably. According to mission records, by 1800 California possessed 74,000 cattle, and by 1833, 424,000.

Spain maintained control of California until 1822, when the province came under Mexican rule. During this period hides and tallow were the chief sources of revenue for the missions. These were sold to New England shipowners who traded them for utensils, plows, hardware, cotton, shoes, underwear, tea, coffee, sugar, and other groceries. No actual money changed hands, because currency and coins were very scarce. A cowhide was known as a "California banknote."

In 1833, disaster struck the missions. A secularization law wrenched the vast, princely land holdings from the missions, and laid them open to private ownership. Before these large claims were parceled out to individual land grants, or *ranchos* ranging in size from 4,500 to 50,000 acres each, the missions slaughtered most of the cattle, and sold the hides and tallow to the shipowners.

According to one eyewitness, the wholesale slaughter, or *matanza,* was well organized: "Six men rode at full speed over the fields, armed with knives. Passing near an animal, one gave it a blow with the knife in the nerve at the nape of the neck, and it fell dead. These *muqueadores* (killers) passed on, and were followed as by a flock of hungry vultures, by dozens of *peladores* (skinners) who took off the hides. Next came the *tasajeros,* who cut up the meat into *tasajo* and *pulpa* (jerked beef and solid beef); and the funeral procession was closed by a swarm of Indian women, who gathered the tallow and lard in leathern hampers. The fat was afterwards rendered out in large iron or copper kettles, and after cooling somewhat was put in skin *botas,* containing on an average of 20 *arrobas,* or 500 pounds."

The hides were staked out to dry in the sun. Next they were doubled over lengthwise, with the hair side in, and piled on carts to be delivered to the small boats which transported them to the larger vessels. These, in turn, delivered them to the curing depot at San Diego. There the flinty hides were soaked in sea water, and once more staked out on the ground. Any particles of flesh or fat were cut away with a knife. Two days later the grease that had oozed out was scraped off. Next the hides were beaten with flails to remove the dust, and stored in a warehouse until time to be loaded for the four to five month voyage around Cape Horn to Boston.

As many *ranchos* came into being through land grants, the carefree owners ushered in a golden age of Spanish ranch life. The aristocratic owners led a life of sumptuous ease, leaving the management of the properties to their *mayordomos*. The livestock roamed the terrain, unfenced because timber was too scarce and expensive, and barbed-wire not yet invented. Indians did all the ranch work, with each ranch supporting several hundred people. It produced its own grain, vegetables, cheese, wine, wool, and meat, and grazed thousands of sheep, cattle, and swine. Indians cooked, cleaned, made butter and cheese, harness and shoes, combed wool, herded, baked, laundered, gardened, and constructed the adobe and timber buildings.

Each *ranchero*, or owner, was required to brand his cattle, and conduct an annual *rodeo*, or beef roundup, in which his neighbors took part. In southern California these roundups were held from April 1 to July 31; farther north, from March to September. They were not festive shows as today with parades and roping and riding contests. They were working roundups, at which time the strayed cattle were gathered into individual herds, branded, tallied, and returned to their home grounds, from which they invariably wandered. The *mayordomo* actually conducted the *rodeo*, with the help of some twenty riders, or *vaqueros*. These highly skilled horsemen received twelve to fifteen dollars a month, and crude living quarters, plus their food, horses, saddle, and ropes.

Each ranch had its own *caballada*, or band of carefully-trained horses in rounding up, roping, cutting, and throwing cattle. Recruited from large bands of wild horses roaming the golden hills, the roundup of wild horses was called a *recogida,* and if anything, was more exciting than the *rodeo* because of the great skill shown by the *vaqueros* in roping the wild steeds and breaking them to saddle.

Of course fresh beef in the form of great ribbed roasts and steaks and succulent stews was a common item on ranch menus. But because of the lack of refrigeration, much of the meat was dried, or "jerked." After a steer was killed, the meat was cut into strips about one inch thick and five or six inches wide, and one to three feet long, and dripped in brine. Then it was hung on a rope in the hot sun, and turned every twenty-four hours. In five days the meat was black, hard, and dry. It was then packed in sixty-pound bales bound with rawhide. Though it looked very unappetizing, the meat tasted good and was nutritious. To cook it, usually it was pounded fine, put in a pan with hot lard, and moistened with water. Then boiled potato and finely cut onion were added along with a generous portion of red chili pepper and tomato, all in all an appetizing dish.

When word of the gold strike near Sacramento in 1849, spread throughout the world, the great stampede to the gold diggings brought thousands of men into California. Because miners worked long hours out of doors, they needed hearty food, and particularly beef. For a few months, the small local supply, augmented with elk and deer, met the demand. Then beef came into very short supply. The *rancheros* to the south suddenly found themselves with a bonanza on their hands. Cattle that would bring only four dollars when slaughtered for hides and tallow now brought fantastically high prices if driven to the mines. Sometimes they sold for seventy-five dollars a head. Hastily herds were shaped up, and driven north along the coastal or interior valleys to San Francisco, Sacramento, or beyond. A few wealthy landowners accompanied their herds at first, but only for the excitement and change of scenery. They left the

actual drudgery of the drive to their workers. There was little loyalty to owner, *mayordomo* or animals, as with the Texas drives. The *vaqueros* were largely inefficient in their herding, though not in their horsemanship. Animals strayed off, stampeded, ate poisonous weeds, or were cut off by Indian or white thieves. No one seemed to be concerned.

The northern cattle buyers and butchers paid for these beeves in gold dust. The suddenly-rich Spanish-Mexican aristocrats busied themselves squandering their new wealth. As Charles Nordhoff wrote in his book *California,* "Saddles trimmed with solid silver, spurs of gold, bridles with silver chains, were among the fancies of the men; and a lady in Santa Barbara amused me by describing the old adobe houses, with earthen floors covered with costly rugs; four-post bedsteads with the costliest lace curtains, and these looped up with lace again; and the senora and senoritas dragging trains of massive silk and satin over the earthen floors. It must have been an odd mixture of squalor and splendor." In addition the newly-rich bought fine china, jewels, ivory-encrusted furniture from the orient, imported wines and tobaccos, and other delicacies. And why not, they would have said. Their ranches were overrun with cattle. The supply was inexhaustible, or so they thought. They took no steps to improve the breed of their cattle, as numerous newly-settled American ranchers were doing already. They also sold too heavily, and did not leave enough seed stock on their land to maintain a natural increase in their herds. Thus by 1850 the supply of cattle in southern California was largely exhausted. The Spanish-Americans, heavily in debt to American money lenders, soon lost their ranches, and many came face to face with real poverty.

The idea of driving beef cattle or work oxen to California spread the length of the inland frontier. From San Antonio, Texas to Milwaukee, Wisconsin, the settlements sent herds to the golden land. Oxen were driven from nearly all parts of the Mississippi Valley and even the Texas coast. Herds were trailed from the Omaha area, from Missouri towns near present-day Kansas City, from the Little Rock-Fort Smith area, from the Indian Nations, as well as from New Mexico, Utah, and Oregon.

Women and children helped drive the oxen hitched to the wagons and the loose herds of extra oxen and milch cows. None, however, helped with any sizable trail herd. The hardships encountered were many. Cholera, measles, scurvy, and smallpox were common among the travelers. Starvation, floods, storms, rattlesnakes, stampedes, rolling rocks, desert sun, quarrels among caravan members, and Indians spelled trouble along the way. The emigrants who depended on oxen faced the danger of having their animals give out from exhaustion, or having them stolen by Indians. Yet in spite of all these difficulties, the people and animals poured into California.

Two main overland trails with numerous branches were used. The Northern Route usually began along the Missouri River, but had branches along the Arkansas. It followed the Platte River across Nebraska into Wyoming, and then cut either through Idaho to Oregon and down into California, or across Utah and Nevada to the gold regions of the north. A second route had branches beginning on the Missouri, the Arkansas, and the Red rivers, and in the San Antonio region of Texas. Still another route led from the Missouri or Arkansas rivers across the plains to Albuquerque, and thence straight across northern Arizona to California. The trail the Texas drovers used began at San Antonio, crossed to the Rio Grande and followed it up and across the mountains into Wyoming to the Northern or Oregon Trail.

The cattle coming into California brought a great change. First, material wealth was added. Transportation got a boost with the coming of oxen capable of hauling wagons. This helped foster the improvement of roads both in the gold regions and the non-mountainous areas. Two new industries started up—the dairy industry, and the raising of beef cattle. This gave employment to men who had not struck it rich, but wanted to stay in California. After the cattle came, there was work for common laborers, cheese makers, bullwhackers, and ranch hands. The presence of an abundant supply of beef cattle allowed the miners extra time for mining gold, and that added to the total of gold gleaned from the gulches. After Americans took over the former Spanish ranches, and Texas cowboys rode the range, even the lackadaisical *vaquero* underwent a change. The Texas cowboys showed him new tricks in handling cattle that revolutionized the business in California.

Of course, as soon as the word spread to Texas that a good strong market for beef cattle existed in California, the Texans weighed their chances. The thought of the profits seemed very bright; the possibility of dangers seemed vague and far-removed. Since this was 1849 and 1850, there was a tremendous supply of Longhorns, and little other activity to fatten the Texas economy. Texans decided to chance it. Their drives northward had gone fairly well, even accounting for the usual dangers. Surely, they argued, the two-thousand mile trek to California wouldn't be much different. Some agreed there might

be a *little* trouble finding water for their stock, and maybe they'd have a run-in with the Comanches or Apaches. Things like that were taken for granted. They'd go well armed, and trust to luck.

As things turned out, the Texans were too optimistic. From end to end the Texas–California trail proved to be one of countless dangers and uncertainties. The long drives set the cattle mad with thirst, and drew saddle horses down to skin and bones. Alkaline lakes and injurious weeds poisoned hundreds of animals. The stony ridges cut their hooves, and Indians made repeated raids, scattering and killing the stock. But the Texans never gave up until after the

Civil War, when the northern markets opened up for them.

T. J. Trimmier of Washington County is credited with pushing the first Texas herd to California. Whenever possible, he followed freighters' and military roads, or old Indian trails. He got one hundred dollars a head for five hundred beeves at the trail's end. Elated, he immediately retraced his route, intending to push through another herd. Incredible as it seems, Trimmier passed herd after herd belonging to fellow Texans bound for the gold country. Of course, as more cattle reached San Francisco and Sacramento, the price broke back to forty dollars a head. Still the Texans came on. They could make a nice profit on beeves that had cost them, at most, fourteen dollars a head back home. Besides, they were desperate for a market.

The traffic on the trail reached its height in 1854. One of the few diaries available of driving cattle from Texas to California was written that year by a young man named James A. Bell. Bell signed on as a rider with a "California cattle train." He was no cowboy, and cared little for cattle. His journal therefore is full of details about the weather, foods, frequent baths, and beautiful sunsets. It gives almost no hint of the troubles the cowhands and cattle had on the long, parched journey. Bell had no loyalty to the drover, and no feeling for the hapless livestock, many of whom died along the way. He was a self-centered traveler, with none of the fine attributes that spelled success for Texans who persevered against terrible odds in pushing their unwieldy herds to market.

All told, over a half million cattle moved westward to California. Thanks to them, miners could eat as well as mine gold; road-building and freighting flourished, and thousands of disappointed gold-seekers turned to ranching and found the bonanza they sought in establishing the state's great cattle industry.

12

Oregon

The Pacific Northwest is a vast region of close-ranked timber, snow-capped mountains, grassy valleys, and long rainy seasons. In the early days it was all called Oregon country, and encompassed a half million square miles now parceled into Oregon, Washington, western Idaho, Montana, and southern British Columbia. Strangely enough, the first cattle known to have set foot in this region probably were Longhorns, and they came by sea rather than land.

Not long after Captain Cook discovered Nootka Sound (near Vancouver Island) in 1778, vessels came to the area bearing settlers and livestock from Monterey, California. Both did well in the damp climate, enough to impress Captain George Vancouver when he explored the coastline some two years later. It occurred to him that it would be wise to establish cattle on the Sandwich Islands, or Hawaii, then a regular calling place for British naval and trading vessels crossing the Pacific. So he set sail for Monterey, took aboard a conglomeration of Spanish livestock, and delivered these to King Kamehameha on the Islands. The king's subjects proved good herders. The fine climate and grass produced an excellent increase in the cattle established on the big island of Hawaii. Not long after, whenever ships from England, Russia, Spain, and the United States called at the islands, the natives came alongside with canoes burdened with fresh fruit, vegetables, and fat young beef.

Meanwhile there was considerable activity up and down the American coast. The Russians had founded a settlement at Fort Ross in northern California, and had a small herd there. In 1811, the fur king, John Jacob Astor, set one expedition of trappers and traders overland to the mouth of the Columbia, and another aboard the *Tonquin* around South America and up the west coast to the mouth of the great river. On board, along with materials and personnel to found a fur post named Astoria, the multi-millionaire Astor included a few head of eastern cattle.

Already the British Hudson's Bay Company had its intrepid trappers gathering furs throughout the region. After a false start or two, in 1825 they founded a fur post called Fort Vancouver some fifty miles up the Columbia. One of the most able men to figure in the history of the Pacific Northwest was placed in charge of this post. He was Dr. John McLoughlin, a tall, genial, fair-minded administrator. Under his guidance, Fort Vancouver acquired a stockade, cannon, many buildings, a sawmill, fields planted to crops, and a burgeoning herd of twenty-seven cows and steers, and three Durham bulls brought from England.

McLoughlin dispensed a firm-handed hospitality to all who called at the fort: Englishmen, Scots, Americans, Irishmen, Islanders, and Indians. When some of the employees wished to retire from the company and acquire farm land, of which there were hundreds of thousands of acres available, he not only released them from service, but gave them on credit, food, equipment, supplies, and two cows and a pair of oxen each. He did not sell the cattle, but loaned them, with the understanding that the new settlers must give back to the fort herd *all* calves produced year after year. Thus by 1835 Fort Vancouver boasted a prosperous 3,000 acre farm, 450 cattle, 200 sheep, 100 horses and 300 hogs. The people at the fort continued to eat wild meat and fowl until 1838, when the good doctor finally gave permission for a beef to be slaughtered for table meat.

The Americans kept coming to Oregon, traders like the unbusiness-like Nathaniel Wyeth, and missionaries like the Reverends Jason and Daniel Lee and Dr. Marcus Whitman. To the Methodist Lees, McLoughlin loaned seven oxen, one bull, and seven cows with calves. Presbyterian Whitman had brought a few head as far west as Fort Hall, in Idaho, but was forced to abandon them there. When he founded his mission near Walla Walla, he too received cattle from Fort Vancouver. The same favor was granted later to Catholic missionaries Father De Smet and Father Demers, who founded missions in present-day Washington, Idaho, and western Montana. As still more forts came into existence, Forts Nisqually, Cowlitz, Okanogan, Walla Walla, Colville, Hall, and Boise, they, too, were stocked with cattle. In time Colville's two cows and bull produced enough so that the smaller fort could equal Fort Vancouver in the production of milk, butter, and beef.

Although the American settlers in Oregon's Willamette Valley (southward across the river from Fort Vancouver) benefited from McLoughlin's generosity and kindness, they returned the favors with criticism. They complained that McLoughlin was trying to keep a stranglehold on the production of cattle in the area. So they got together, along with some disgruntled Canadians, and formed the Willamette Cattle Company. It was organized to trail California cattle into Oregon. Ewing Young, a veteran trail hand, was voted leader, and Philip Edwards the treasurer. Nine Americans and two Canadians signed on as trail herders, and some twenty-five hundred dollars was raised with which to buy the cattle. The small party rode ship to Monterey, and immediately ran afoul of a recent regulation that forbade the export of cattle out of California. Young finally wangled permission to do so from Governor Alvarado at Monterey, although a good bit of the precious money had to be used as bribes before the permission was forthcoming.

Seven weeks dribbled by in many exasperations before the Oregon party acquired eight hundred poor animals, and moved them to the bank of the San Joaquin River. The first night the cattle broke out of the makeshift corral thrown together to hold them, and eighty-two head were lost. Next, crossing the river proved a nightmare. The stubborn cattle simply would not take to the water. Even though the herder towed the calves across, few cows would follow. Some would venture out to midstream, then panic, mill, and flounder back. Seventeen animals drowned. The men fashioned rafts of bullrushes, fastened a line to a tree on the opposite bank, and pulled a beast or two over on the makeshift raft. They also tried tightening ropes around the cattle's horns, and literally dragging them across. Seven difficult days passed before the dangerous task was completed.

Almost the last animal to be taken over was the pack mule bearing the party's total supply of ammunition. The mule took fright, plunged and rolled, thoroughly soaking the powder. There was nothing to do but tarry on the mosquito-infested banks while two men rode back sixty miles to buy more ammunition and rejoin their party. And Oregon was still five hundred miles distant!

The following three months were almost as bad. The men quarreled among themselves; they cussed the cattle; they floundered over other rivers and scaled impassable mountains. But finally, they reached the Willamette Valley wih 630 young cows and bulls. Members of the stock company rationed the cattle among themselves. They turned them out, largely unattended, to graze on the thick grass. So, in spite of the hardship and aggravations, the long drive up from California had accomplished its purposes; it freed the Willamette settlers of their dependence on the Fort Vancouver herd, and brought new livestock into the region.

Not to be outdone, in 1844 the Hudson's Bay Company formed a subsidiary called the Puget Sound Agricultural Company, and imported 2,000 head of cattle and 4,000 sheep from California. These swelled the herds at various company posts. But an even greater influx of cattle occurred in and after 1843 when emigrants blazed the Oregon Trail and streamed into the Oregon country. One company of 1,000 persons and 120 wagons brought 5,000 head from Independence, Missouri to the Willamette Valley, a distance of two thousand miles. An estimated 1,500 persons with cattle came in the next year, and 3,000 more in 1845. By 1848, one historian wrote that the Willamette Valley was "covered with the herds of cattle."

Oregon profited from the good shorthorn cattle brought in during the great migrations of the 1840's and 1850's. Her winters bred strong, rugged animals. By this time almost every part of Oregon had herds ranging in size for a few hundred to several thousand head. Pendleton and John Day became famed cattle centers. (Pendleton still is the scene annually of one of the world's best rodeos.) East of the Blue Mountains, La Grande and Baker were major cattle markets, with Bend and Prineville dominating the business on the east slope of the Cascade Mountains.

Starting in the 1860's, the third and fourth generation descendants of the cattle that had come west on the Oregon Trail began moving eastward to stock the ranges of northern Idaho, Montana and Wyoming. Product of midwestern shorthorns and quality Devon bulls, they were sturdy, fat animals possessing more beef on the hoof than the best Longhorns. They were called "American" cattle, to differentiate them from the California and Texas stock. How these cattle got to Montana and Wyoming, and even the Dakotas, is a trail story that equals in hardship any drive north from Texas. But it is a story writers have neglected almost entirely and is therefore little known.

Montana had received her first cattle as early as 1850. That year Captain Richard Grant and his two sons traded along the emigrant road in Utah for footsore, worn-out cattle and horses. Usually these animals were of good quality, and needed only rest and good grass to bring them back to top form. So, after gathering up a sizable herd of these weary pilgrims, Grant drove them northward to graze in the mountain-hemmed valleys of western Montana. Then in the spring he trailed them back to Utah, and exchanged them at considerable profit, one fat animal for two trail-worn ones. Other men soon were engaged in this activity, and cattle were trailed to the luxuriant grass of Montana's Jefferson, Beaverhead, Deer Lodge, and Stinking-water valleys. (The Stinkingwater is now more elegantly called the Ruby.) Meantime Father Pierre Jean De Smet had come west with an emigrant train, left it at Fort Hall, and with a small group founded a mission among the Flathead Indians in the Bitterroot valley. With seeds and milch cows brought over from Fort Colville, a Hudson's Bay post on the Columbia, the good priest developed a flourishing mission. But the Blackfeet Indians made so much trouble that Father De Smet finally sold the mission property to a "Major" John Owen. Under Owen's guidance, the layout soon became a fine cattle ranch.

In 1853 the brand new governor of the Washington Territory, Isaac I. Stevens, headed a survey party which sought a railroad route from Minneapolis to Seattle. After a good pass was discovered through the jumbled peaks of western Montana, a road was built from the headwaters of navigation on the Missouri at Fort Benton, Montana Territory, westward 624 miles to a post at the Dalles on the Columbia. Soon cattle began moving eastward over this improved Mullan Trail, named for the young lieutenant who superintended its construction, and Montana's western valleys received more Oregon livestock.

In 1862, 1863, and 1864, three rousing gold strikes at Bannack, Virginia City, and Last Chance Gulch (Helena) brought tens of thousands of men to the Montana diggings. Not all of them struck it rich on their gold placers. A fair number, noting the beautiful valleys roundabout, stayed and established cattle ranches. Much of the stock they brought in came from Oregon. The herds usually were shaped up at Baker. It took a month or more to round up the horses, break them to saddle and shoe them, and road brand the 2,000 three- and four-year-old steers. Five days out the herds gathered on the bank of a treacherous river. This deep, swift stream was a brute, compared to the Red and Arkansas rivers of the south. It was called the Snake. The herders carefully worked the cattle out onto a long sand bar jutting into the powerful current. On the far bank, a ferryman brought his few cows to the river to drink, so they could serve as decoys. Then the point riders, yelling like crazy, drove the leaders into the water. Seeing the cows on the far side, they were less reluctant about plunging in and swimming across. The rest of the herd and men had little trouble making it over.

Ahead lay rough-and-tumble, up-and-down mountain country with sparse grass. The hands rode hard, yelled, cracked their whips, and after a dry spell, got the herds to the Weiser River. Because they were thirsty, the cattle went in without protest. Another long drive

brought them to the Payette River. Here, on one occasion, a pack
of dogs from an Indian village stampeded the cattle. It took a lot of
riding to get things straightened out, and a number of the dogs were
shot in the excitement. Invariably, since it was now July or August,
electrical storms hit the outfits. The cattle milled and bawled, but
didn't stampede because the ground was covered with coarse lava
rock that cut their hooves. A sand bar on the Boise River made that

an easy river to cross. Then came two torturous days of plodding through lava rock and ash. The heat radiating off the rock cooked men and stock alike. The cattle stirred up clouds of dust which clogged and burned their eyes and noses, and those of the horses and riders. The only water available was in small holes, and was too brackish to drink. The cattle's tongues began to hang out; they moaned and bawled, and tried to turn in every direction. But the riders kept yelling and firing their revolvers, and by nightfall of the second night, the lead steers sniffed water. One of the many loops of the Snake River lay ten miles ahead. Now the problem was to hold back each herd, in order to keep it from plunging over twenty-foot banks to get to the water. Hard riding and stringing the cattle out in a long line averted disaster. From there it was comparatively easy going to a mountain divide leading into Montana.

Thousands upon thousands of cattle were pointed east along the Oregon Trail to Boise, across Little Camas and Big Camas prairies and the Giant Lava Beds (now Craters of the Moon National Monument), a hundred miles of lava wasteland, to Blackfoot or Eagle Falls (now Idaho Falls), and north over gentle Monida Pass into Montana. Others took a slightly different and almost paralleling route beyond Boise called the Northern Trail. East of Eagle Falls they were wintered close to Gray's Lake, then angled up the easy sage-brush-covered slope of South Pass, and dropped down into Wyoming's vast central grasslands.

Quite a few Oregon herds also wintered in Montana, where they came through surprisingly well, and then were driven down the Yellowstone River either to Dakota, or northward into Canada. Still others followed a Yellowstone tributary, the Clark Fork, southward over the mountains into the magnificent valley of the Big Horn. In the six years, 1869 to 1875, which embraced the heavy flow from west to east, over a quarter million cattle streamed out of Oregon. Actually the extremes of heat and cold, the booming Snake River, the thirst and glass-edged lava would wreak greater hardship on men and animals than the weary miles from Texas to Kansas. However, the Oregon-east movement would contribute something ultimately more important by establishing sturdier, beefier short-horns on the Montana and Wyoming ranges. In four decades, they would supplant the skinny-flanked, thin-skinned Longhorns yet to come up the Texas-Montana Trail.

As Charles W. Towne and Edward N. Wentworth wrote in their book *Cattle and Men,* "Written history fails to confer recognition on these Northwestern herds. Historians dealing with this period have been more interested in telling of missions, churches, schools, music, minerals, railroads and theaters." They have not given credit to the cattle who brought prosperity to the Pacific Northwest, and enabled the hardy pioneers to change a wilderness into five great states.

13

The Texas-Montana Trail

Gold!

The hoarse cry had drawn thousands to California in 1849, and to Colorado in the 1850's. Now it was being hollered from the gulches of Montana in the early spring of 1863.

Nelson Story heard the news when it raced by word of mouth through Colorado. He was a young man, only twenty-five, with a nice business freighting goods between Denver and Leavenworth, Kansas. Thus he was no stranger to plains weather, blizzards, Indian attacks, and hard work.

On hearing the good news of the gold strike, Story realized immediately that the Montana diggings would be a mighty good place to market flour, coffee, cured pork, molassas, kettles, bolts of cloth, gold pans and shovels, underwear, and other necessities. Gold miners would pay high prices for such staples, since thousands stampeded to gold discoveries with little thought of where or how they would obtain food and other supplies.

Accordingly, this quiet but courageous young man loaded two wagons with goods, yoked on sturdy ox teams, and in addition added a string of eleven pack mules, also burdened with supplies. With two helpers and his wife, Story set out on the well-worn road to Corinne,

Utah, and then turned north to Bannack, the scene of the first big Montana gold discovery. When he arrived in early June, he found the camp all but deserted! But it didn't take long to find out why. A newer, richer gold strike had been located sixty miles to the east, in Alder Gulch. Already ten thousand men had hurried to the new bonanza.

"I've got to move on to Alder Gulch," Story told his young wife. "A new gold camp is no place for a young woman. If I can find a place for you, will you stay in Bannack for a while?"

Although Ellen did not like being separated from her husband, she had heard tales about the rough goings-on in gold camps. "I'll stay," she agreed.

Soon Ellen was housed comfortably with a nice family. Story left his wagons and oxen in Bannack, and set out with his loaded pack string. When he and his men got to the narrow, twisting gulch that was staked off into gold claims for miles up and down each side of the creek, he set up store in a hastily-thrown together building. He made a fat profit selling his goods. He even had time to locate a gold claim of his own. As soon as he could have a cabin built, he returned to Bannack, picked up the remainder of the goods and his wife, and moved back to the town that had sprung up at the discovery. It was called Virginia City. Ellen helped in the store, and made berry, dried apple, and pumpkin pies for which the miners paid five dollars in gold dust. The young couple prospered.

But Story still was not satisfied. A man who looked ahead, he realized that the miners in Virginia City would need a great deal of meat during the following winter, and that the elk, deer, moose, and bear in the neighboring mountains were already being shot out of existence. Also, there very well could be a near famine if he and other storekeepers ran out of flour. Now, if he were really smart, he told himself, he would bring both cattle and flour to the gold camp.

"But won't it take more money than we have?" Ellen asked when he discussed the idea with her.

Story nodded. He would need much more money than he had accumulated so far. "I haven't worked the gold claim yet. I'll give it a try." Gathering together a gold pan, pick and shovel from his own store, Story set to work panning the gravel along his creek-side claim. In a short time he had panned out sixty thousand dollars worth of gold nuggets!

Story deposited half of his gold in the bank vault for safekeeping. Then he hammered together a stout strong box, put thirty thousand dollars worth of gold in it, and rode with it by stagecoach to Salt Lake City, Utah. From there he dispatched the gold by Wells Fargo Express coach to a New York City bank. He followed by stage and railroad, and in New York converted his gold to greenbacks, or paper currency, realizing a profit of ten thousand dollars this way. He sewed ten thousand dollars worth of the currency inside his suit coat lining, and took a bank letter of credit for the remaining amount. Then he went west to Leavenworth, Kansas and deposited the letter of credit in a bank in order to open a checking account.

A short time later Story met two trusted friends whom he had known when he was freighting between Leavenworth and Denver. "Billy Petty! Tom Allen!" he called them by name. After much talk, he said, "How about going to Texas with me? I'm going down there to buy a herd of cattle and drive it up to Montana."

"Sure thing," they answered. "How soon do we start?"

"Right now," he told them, laughing.

The three young men reached Fort Worth, Texas in June of 1866. After visiting several ranches in the area, Story bought one thousand good steers and cows.

"Where are you goin' to push 'em?" the ranchers asked.

"To Montana," Story answered.

The ranchers shook their heads. Anyone with an ounce of sense would know that it was impossible to drive Longhorns that far, twenty-five hundred miles! For a greenhorn like Story to try it was sheer folly.

Story just smiled, and went about his business. As soon as he had enough cattle and horses, he hired twenty-two more riders. Several were in their late teens, but all were veterans of the War Between the States. They could be counted on to ride well, work hard, and if necessary, to fight. One of them was a crusty old-timer who claimed he made the lightest biscuits in Texas. He was hired to cook, and drive the wagon that hauled the food, gear, and bedrolls. It took several days to round up the cattle, run them through a chute, and road-brand them. At last, early in August, Story mounted a chunky black horse, waved his hat, and hollered, "Start 'em moving!"

The point, swing, flank, and drag riders were already in their places. The cook snapped the reins over his four mules, and started the wagon rolling. The outfit hit the trail. At first the steers and cows were ornery, and tried to turn back. Story kept a stiff pace for three days. Each night the stock tried to bolt. But finally they paired off, and settled down. It was a noisy procession, the cattle bawling, their horns clattering, their hooves pounding the turf. The cowboys yelled and swung their ropes. In the rear, the drag riders cracked their whips incessantly. The horse wrangler with his *remuda* of extra horses rode out to the side of the herd. Only Story was far in front, setting the direction and locating good camp sites.

North from Fort Worth, he followed a well-trod trail to the Red River. Here Story got his first initiation in crossing a flood-swollen river. As soon as the lead animals caught up with him at the river bank, he spurred his horse, yelled and plunged into the water. The point riders whipped their ropes over the leaders' heads. By this time, they were so crowded by others pressing them from the rear that they had no choice but to plunge in.

Instinctively the animals followed Story, who kept swinging his hat so they could see him. The riders pressed the cattle so they swarmed into the water. They looked strange—wild-eyed, snorting, hooves churning, at times only their noses and horns above water. They made the far shore, and for a few moments stood spraddle-legged, their flanks heaving. Then a few began to nibble at the grass, and before long the entire herd stopped bawling and grazed. Some of the men returned to the south shore to build a makeshift raft so the cook wagon could be ferried over. With that done, Story heaved a sigh of relief. He had crossed his first river without losing a man or an animal.

The herd moved on to Baxter Springs, Missouri. After buying more supplies there, Story continued on up through the Indian Nations. When several Indians stopped him and demanded a toll payment of ten cents a head, Story gulped. But he paid promptly. Some of his riders objected. They wanted to pull their guns, and bull their way through. Story would have none of this. His cattle were eating grass that belonged to the Indians. He felt he should pay.

One night a storm threatened. At the first clap of thunder and flash of lightning, the herd took off. It took hard riding the remainder of the night to keep them from scattering in six directions.

They crossed the Canadian and North Canadian rivers easily but ran into trouble with quicksand at the Cimarron. By the time Story and his crew had freed twenty trapped steers and crossed the river, they were so tired they dropped exhausted. Yet within an hour all were on the way again.

Then real trouble in the form of a party of swaggering, tough-looking armed riders appeared in extreme southeastern Kansas.

"Who's the boss of this herd?" their leader demanded.

"I am," Story spoke up.

"We're agents for the Grangers' Association. We don't want your tick-ridden critters crossin' our country. We're tellin' you to turn back."

Story knew the men were not grangers. He had been warned about this in Fort Worth. They were Jayhawkers, those murderous guerillas who stole cattle. "What if I don't turn back?" he said.

The outlaw pointed his gun at Story, "Wa'll if you pay us three dollars a head toll fee, I reckon we'll let you pass."

Story thought it over. This was outrageous blackmail. If his way north was barred by one such group of outlaws, it could be barred by others. His main job was to get his herd through. But he would not pay highway robbery, and yet he had no intention of getting into a gunfight with the larger party of Jayhawkers.

"Turn back," he told his riders.

Some objected. They'd rather fight. But Story was the boss. When he said to turn back, they followed orders. Story moved further west, and located a new passage northward to the Nebraska line. Because this was sparsely settled country, there was no further trouble.

Once the herd was pointed for the Oregon Trail, Story put it in charge of Petty and Allen, and rode alone east to Leavenworth. Here he purchased three wagons, twelve span of oxen, and several tons of flour and other supplies. He also bought thirty of the new, fast-firing Remington rifles. Although not repeating rifles, they could be fired as much as seventeen times a minute. They were the fastest guns in the West. Story bought plenty of ammunition for them. A week later Story, his wagons, and bullwhackers had rejoined the herd.

They paralleled the Union Pacific Railroad as far as Grand Island, Nebraska and then trailed on across the Platte River to Fort Laramie, Wyoming. There, while his teams and herd rested, Story announced his intention of taking the Bozeman Road into Montana. This was a shortcut northwest through Sioux territory that was several hundred miles shorter than the heavier-traveled route farther west. When the Army officers stationed at the fort heard what he had in mind, they advised him to forget about the Bozeman Road. The ferocious Sioux were on the warpath that fall. His chances of running the gauntlet with a slow-moving herd were very slim.

Story talked it over with his men. With their new rifles to protect them, they were willing to try the shortcut. Story gave the order to move out. The cut-off was well marked. There were military posts along the way. By early October, the expedition camped alongside the Powder River. Directly west were the towering snow-capped Big Horn mountains, and to the east the lesser Pumpkin Buttes. The valley was cross-hatched with Indian signs—travoid marks, pony tracks, and round barren circles where tepees had been raised. Story doubled the night guard.

The next day a wagon hove into sight, and not long after a French Canadian trapper and a young lad joined them. The trapper reported that he had not been molested by any Indians so far, and that Fort Reno was only about ten miles distant. He refused Story's offer to join them in camp, and continued on another mile.

Although the night guards were alert, Indians crept close to the herd. At dawn they rushed in, some shooting, others flapping blankets and spooking the cattle. Before the cowboys could leap to their horses, the Indians managed to cut off about twenty head of cattle, and drive them away up a coulee nearby. The cowmen were too busy trying to control the herd to follow them. The shots had started a stampede, and also injured two of the Texans.

It took hours to restore order and get the herd quieted down. Even then Story would not rest. With several of his men, he pursued the raiders. Their tracks were easy to follow. At dusk they came onto their camp. Apparently the Indians had not expected to be followed. They had killed a steer and were having a feast. When Story and his men cut loose with the new guns, several Indians died. The others raced off in the dark.

The cowmen rounded up their cattle and returned to the herd. Thinking the trappers might like some of the meat retrieved from the Indian camp, Story and some of his men rode over to their wagon. They found the two had been scalped and multilated, and the wagon and furs torn to pieces. After giving them a decent burial, Story once more set his outfit on the road.

The next day the long caravan moved on to Fort Reno. It was a small post with cottonwood log and mud-chinked buildings enclosed behind a stockade. Captain Joshua Proctor, in charge of the badly-undermanned fort, told Story it was useless to continue on through the Sioux country. He said the Indians were on the prowl, and already had run off all the fort's horses and cattle. In spite of this, and after leaving his two wounded men there to recover from their wounds, Story moved on to Fort Kearny. It was situated near Big Pincy Creek at the foot of a great peak. The post consisted of some thirty sturdy buildings which housed barracks, officers' quarters, kitchen, guardhouse, hospital, and stables. But it was six miles from the nearest firewood, and the parties dispatched from the fort to cut wood were under constant attack. Colonel Henry M. Carrington ordered Story to turn back to the Oregon Trail.

"Why?" Story demanded.

Carrington said he had orders to turn back any outfit that numbered less than forty men. Since no additional outfits were apt to come along this late in the season, Story would have to turn back.

Story explained he had twenty-seven veterans, all armed with new Remingtons. Carrington refused to change his orders. And, because grass around the post was needed for the military animals, he ordered Story to move his outfit three miles out from the post!

Story knew better than to argue, even though it was obvious his men and animals would be subject to attack. Once more he talked over the situation with his men, and once more they all agreed to go on, with or without permission of the military. So, after dark, the outfit pulled out, walked all night, and during the next day hid as much as possible in some willow thickets along a stream.

By this time the mountains were white with fresh snow, the cottonwoods had turned yellow, and there was ice atop the water buckets every morning. The Texas cowboys were feeling the cold. Story issued extra clothing, and also handfuls of cartridges for the rifles. By trailing only through the dark, and hiding out in the daytime, Story brought his outfit across the danger-ridden miles from the Big Horn Mountains in Wyoming on north to the Big Horn River in Montana. Here a blizzard hit them. The cattle began to drift ahead of the storm. The riders, huddled in jackets and with kerchiefs tying their hats down around their ears, were unable to turn the stock. They drifted with them all night and the next day. Eventually the storm blew out so the cattle could be worked back to the trail. Some of the cowboys were so chilled that they had to be helped from their saddles. Soon all thawed out around crackling campfires.

The storm had brought one advantage: the Indians had holed up in their tepees. Story had no more trouble reaching a good ford near the mouth of the Stillwater River, near present-day Columbus,

Montana. On December 1, a big valley opened up ahead. There were mountains on the south, west, and north, and plenty of grass, water, and wood. It was a perfect spot for a ranch. Story called a halt. He had his men saw logs for buildings and corrals. After cutting out a small herd of prime steers, he took a few of his riders and the wagons on into Virginia City. On December 9, practically the whole gold camp turned out to celebrate the arrival of the Texas herd, and to toast Story for having completed the longest cattle drive in history. Thanks to his foresight and courage, Virginia City did not lack either meat or flour that winter. The Story ranch would operate well into the 1900's.

Usually when some intrepid pathfinder opens the way, others follow. This was not the case here. When the Sioux resumed prowling in the spring of 1867, they halted all traffic on the Bozeman Road. Some outfits gambled, but none got through, and their bones and graves lined the way. In fact, for eight more years, the Indians throttled settlement of eastern Wyoming and Montana. Although cattle poured from the Oregon Trail into the western portion of both territories, there were none in the valleys of the Powder, Big Horn, and Yellowstone rivers.

Finally in 1876, the Sioux signed a treaty, and withdrew to a reservation in Dakota. The following spring a half million cattle came up Story's Texas-Montana Trail, and poured like a flood over the grassy range. They spread out from the Platte on the south to the Canadian border on the north. In spite of the tick embargo in Kansas, they kept coming. But as the Union Pacific and Northern Pacific railroads reached further out across the plains, more and more cattle came west by rails, than afoot. These were largely Herefords, superior cattle that would rustle for grass under snow. They fared much better than the Longhorns, and within twenty years supplanted the southern cattle. The Texas cowboys liked the north better, in spite of the cold winters. Many settled down on small ranches, or signed on with big cattle outfits.

The combination of free grass, limitless unfenced public domain,

freedom from ticks and other bothersome insects, and a strong demand for cattle throughout the midwest and east proved irresistible.
Many people in the United States and abroad, particularly Eng-

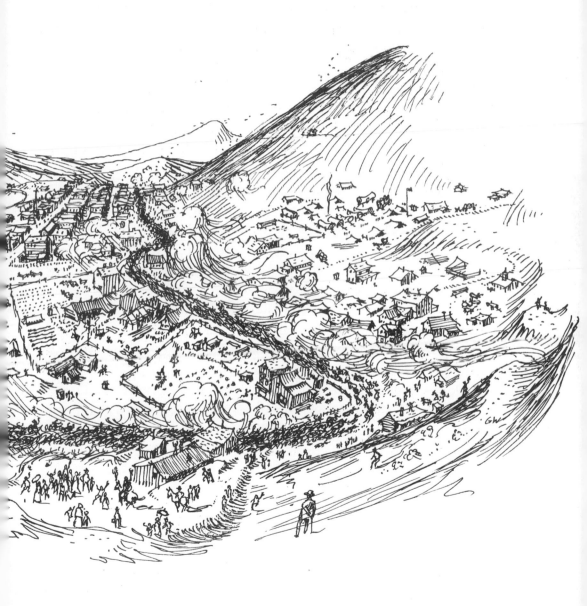

land, who had never set foot on a ranch invested money in large cattle companies that ran hundreds of thousands of cattle on the Montana-Wyoming range. At first the profits were staggering. But the grass was not inexhaustible, as every one thought. It became over-cropped. A long hot, dry summer and numerous grass fires in the fall of 1886 worsened conditions. Cattle went into winter without sufficient feed. Then early in December, one of the greatest blizzards of recorded history locked the plains in an icy grip for long weeks. When the snow finally thawed, months later, the gulleys and foothills were dotted with stinking carcasses. Many cattle companies went bankrupt. Other operators were reduced to a few hundred head. The day of the open range cattle business was over. After that, barbed wire, fenced pastures, haystacks, and smaller herds brought a sturdy rebirth to the cattle industry on the plains.

By this time, trailing cattle overland was impractical. There were herds in every section of the United States, enough to meet the constantly growing demand for beef and its by-products. Cattle moved quicker and more easily across the country on railroads. The long drive went out of existence. Now, the only drives were from the ranch gate to the railroad. Then even these short drives disappeared when large, lumbering cattle trucks picked up the steers and cows at the ranch gate, and transported them to the nearest stockyards. No longer did cattle move up from Texas, or back down the Oregon Trail. The mountain and northwest states boasted self-sufficient herds, and this last frontier of trailing closed the final chapter in the story of America's cattle trails, east and west.

Bibliography

Abbott, E. C., *We Pointed Them North*. New York, Farrar & Rinehart, 1939.

Adams, A., *The Log of a Cowboy*. Boston, Houghton Mifflin, 1931.

American Heritage, *Adventures in the Wilderness*. New York, American Heritage, 1963.

American Heritage, *American Heritage Book of Indians*. New York, American Heritage, 1961.

Andrews, C. M., *The Colonial Period of American History*. New Haven, Yale University Press, 1934.

Applegate, Jesse, *A Day with the Cow Column in 1843*. Chicago, Caxton Club, 1934.

Beck, Warren A., *New Mexico: A History of Four Centuries*. Norman, University of Oklahoma Press, 1962.

Bell, James G., *A Log of the Texas-California Trail, 1854*. In Southwestern Historical Quarterly, 1932.

Brayer, H. O. and G. M., *American Cattle Trails*. Bayside, New York, American Pioneer Trails Association, 1952.

Burt, S., *Powder River, Let 'Er Buck*. New York, Farrar & Rinehart, 1938.

Chapman, C. E., *A History of California: The Spanish Period*. New York, Macmillan, 1921.

Cleland, R. G., *The Cattle on a Thousand Hills*. San Marino, California, The Huntington Library, 1941.

Cureton, G., *The Cattle Trail to California, 1840–1860*. In *Quarterly*, Historical Society of Southern California, June, 1953.

Dacy, G. H., *Four Centuries of Florida Ranching*. St. Louis, the author, 1940.

De Kruif, Paul, *Microbe Hunters*. New York, Harcourt Brace, 1926.

Dixon, Olive K., *The Life of Billy Dixon*. Dallas, P. L. Turner, 1940.

Dobie, F. J., *The Longhorns*. Boston, Little, Brown, 1941.

Drago, H. S., *Great American Cattle Trails*. New York, Dodd Mead, 1965.

Fisher, M., *Colonial America*. Grand Rapids, Michigan, Fideler, 1962.

Flack, Captain A., *A Hunter's Experiences in the Southern States of America.* London, Longmans Green, 1860.

Gard, W., *The Chisholm Trail.* Norman, University of Oklahoma Press, 1954.

Grant, B., *Longhorn.* New York, World, 1956.

Haley, J. E., *Charles Goodnight, Cowman and Plainsman.* Norman, University of Oklahoma Press, 1949.

Hanna, C. A., *The Wilderness Trail.* New York, Putnam, 1911, 2 vols.

Hebard, G. R. and Brininstool, E. A., *The Bozeman Trail.* Cleveland, Arthur H. Clark, 1922.

McCoy, J. G., *Historic Sketches of the Cattle Trade of the West and Southwest.* Glendale, California, Arthur H. Clark, 1940.

Osgood, E. S., *The Day of the Cattleman.* Minneapolis, University of Minnesota Press, 1954.

Pelzer, L., *The Cattlemen's Frontier.* Glendale, California, Arthur H. Clark, 1936.

Sandoz, M., *The Cattleman.* New York, Hastings House, 1958.

Stuart, G., *Forty Years on the Frontier,* Vol. 2. Cleveland, Arthur H. Clark, 1925.

Thompson, J. W., *History of livestock raising in the United States, 1607–1860.* U.S. Dept. Agriculture, Agricultural History Series, No. 5, Washington, 1942.

Towne, C. W., and Wentworth, E. N., *Cattle and Men.* Norman, University of Oklahoma Press, 1955.

Wellman, P. I., *The Trampling Herd.* New York, Doubleday, 1952.

Index